midcentury
modern style

midcentury modern style

AN APPROACHABLE GUIDE TO INSPIRED ROOMS

KAREN NEPACENA

Photographs by Christopher Dibble

Gibbs Smith

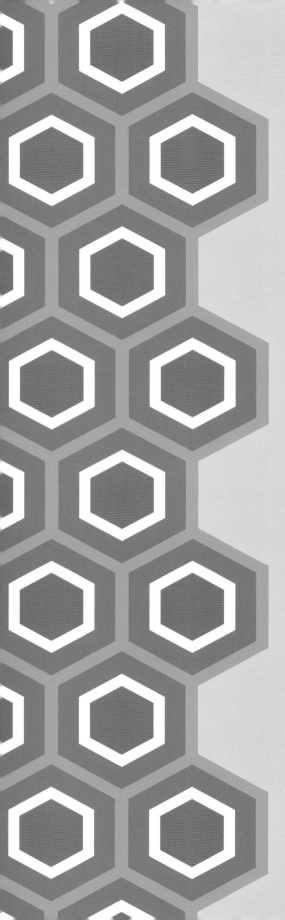

First Edition
26 25 24 23   5 4 3 2

Published by
Gibbs Smith
P.O. Box 667
Layton, Utah 84041
1.800.835.4993 orders
www.gibbs-smith.com

Cover and interior designer: Patricia Fabricant
Art director: Ryan Thomann
Editor: Gleni Bartels
Production designer: Virginia Snow
Production editor: Sue Collier
Production manager: Felix Gregorio

Printed and bound in Shenzhen, China, by Elegance Printing (SZ) Ltd.
Gibbs Smith books are printed on either recycled, 100%
post-consumer waste, FSC-certified papers or on paper
produced from sustainable PEFC-certified forest/controlled
wood source. Learn more at www.pefc.org.

Library of Congress Control Number: TK
ISBN: 978-1-4236-6395-9

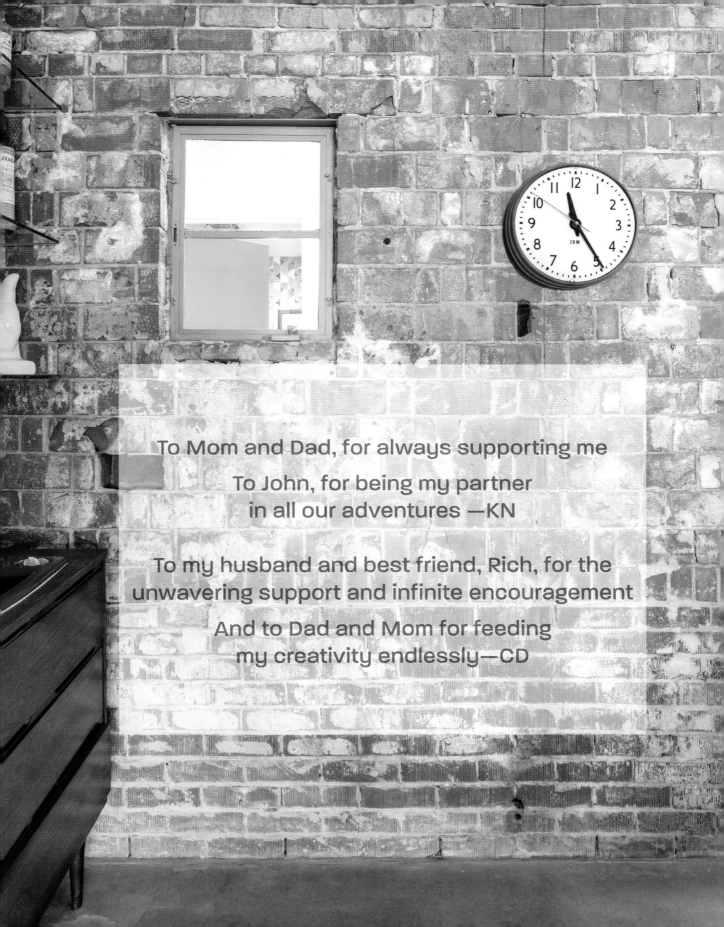

To Mom and Dad, for always supporting me

To John, for being my partner
in all our adventures —KN

To my husband and best friend, Rich, for the
unwavering support and infinite encouragement

And to Dad and Mom for feeding
my creativity endlessly—CD

CONTENTS

INTRODUCTION

My first encounter with midcentury modern design was a love-at-first-sight kind of moment. At the time, my husband, John, and I owned a 1970s ranch-style home. We had renovated it ourselves and had no intention of moving. But at the urging of our friend and real estate agent, Angie, we went to a nearby open house for a midcentury modern home built by the post–World War II real estate developer Joseph Eichler. The home, or "Eichler" as they are called, had an interior atrium courtyard and spans of glass windows. It was a house that was modern and cool yet homey and functional at the same time. That was it. I wanted to live in that feeling, and I didn't even know what it was I was experiencing.

We didn't buy that house, but we did eventually find an Eichler to make our own. But its state was far from the dreamy version we had toured before. Nearly every midcentury modern detail had been removed or replaced. The home was void of the original spans of floor-to-ceiling windows, and the wood-pinstripe exterior siding had been replaced with a vinyl variation. Our house had a cottage-style feel, totally absent of any midcentury modern charm. It just wouldn't do. So my husband and I started researching the particular details of the design and build of Eichler homes, and over the course of several years, slowly brought our midcentury modern home back to its roots.

Just as I stumbled into midcentury modern design, I also fell into interior design as a career. During our home renovation, John and I journaled our projects on a blog we called Destination Eichler, named after our long search for our Eichler home. During this period my love, appreciation, and passion for all things midcentury modern really manifested. Over time, we began to receive inquiries from others asking for design help to transform and restore their

Christopher Dibble (right) and me on a shoot for the book in Stanford, CA.

midcentury homes. I eventually quit my day job in e-commerce product management to take on interior design clients full time. It was a big (and scary!) leap, but I've never looked back.

We've since transformed from a DIY blog to a full-service boutique interior design firm, through which I have helped over 150 clients restore, renovate, or furnish their homes—from original Eichlers and custom-built midcentury modern homes to Craftsman houses, lofts, ranch homes, and condos. What started off as a one-woman design shop has developed into a small but mighty team of four, who create new designs for our growing list of mid-mod-loving clientele. Our interior design work has been featured in *Domino*, *Dwell*, *HGTV Magazine*, and *Atomic Ranch*, and, despite my nontraditional design background and DIY roots, I am seen as an expert in the field of midcentury modern design.

Photographer Christopher Dibble and I met serendipitously via Instagram. He introduced himself and expressed his openness to photograph my work in the future. A few months later, after completing one of my first large-scale midcentury modern residential projects in the Bay Area, I contacted him to take him up on his offer. He agreed, flew down for a day to photograph the renovation, and a great designer-photographer partnership formed. Chris creates beautiful images that represent the vibrancy and spirit of my work and has photographed my design projects from California to Arizona to Vermont. One day, we came up with the idea to publish an interior design book that married the spirit and sleekness of midcentury modern design with an approachable, everyday sensibility, and *Midcentury Modern Style* was born!

I love poring over architecture books, visiting original buildings, going on midcentury home tours, and discovering finishing details that are not often seen in new building construction or current-day mass-furniture manufacturing. I get so much joy and satisfaction from using what I've learned to create or re-create these ideas in my work. I strive to make the spaces I design for clients truly livable and comfortable. Yes, I want their homes to look beautiful, but they also need to be practical and functional for real life. Clients tell me they don't want to feel like they live in a museum but in a home and, more importantly, *their* home. This book came from the idea that your home—and any room—can be inspired by the midcentury modern aesthetic and still exude warmth and life.

1 | MIDCENTURY MODERN MAGIC, THEN AND NOW

During the real-estate boom that took place from the 1930s to the 1960s (the midcentury), developers built mass housing that was designed to meet the needs of middle-class American families after World War II. Large neighborhoods of modest-sized, affordable-to-build homes started popping up in the suburbs of American cities. Not surprisingly, these homes offered a front yard and a backyard, giving more room for the kids to play, and a carport or garage. Inside there was typically a small, often galley-shaped kitchen, a family room and/or a formal living room, a dining area, a handful of bedrooms (used only for sleeping, so they weren't very large), and a bathroom or two—all built for the traditional nuclear family of the time: mom, dad, and two or three kids. Despite their cookie-cutter description, many of these houses were designed by renowned architects, such as A. Quincy Jones, William Krisel, and Cliff May and/or were built by modernist real estate developers, such as Joseph Eichler, Henry Doelger, Robert Rummer, Franklin L. Burns, and the Streng Brothers. As a result, these modern, multifunctional, and innovative (for their time) homes were designed with the average postwar American middle-class family in mind.

Then, during the 1980s through the early 2000s, many original midcentury homes started showing their age and wear. Homeowners began upgrading and updating the original architecture in various ways, such as incorporating new and popular building materials, which many times left the original history, materials, and structure in the dust. Original postwar building materials were painted over or replaced with more "contemporary" finishes: Sheetrock replaced wood paneling, paint or popcorn finish smothered handcrafted tongue-and-groove ceilings, contemporary tile or paint colors were layered over original brick or stone fireplaces—the travesty!

Which brings us to today. In recent years, midcentury modern design and architecture has experienced renewed appreciation. Some period-specific television shows, such as *Mad Men* or *The Queen's Gambit,* have likely played a small part in its resurgence, but many enthusiasts (myself included) came to love MCM design because of the clean lines and the minimalism inherent in its home structures, furniture, artwork, graphic design, and housewares. These design features somehow simultaneously create a sense of futuristic possibility and timelessness, so it's no wonder people all over the world are trying to bring a bit of the magic into their homes.

In this midcentury modern "Deck House" in Warren, VT, we preserved as many original architectural elements as possible, from the fireplace to the natural finish of the tongue-and-groove ceilings.

Making Midcentury Modern Your Own

So how can you bring a bit of that midcentury modern magic to your own home? Throughout the coming chapters, I'll take you room by room (and outside), explaining how following just a handful of simple design guideposts, can create the mid-mod space of your dreams.

Transforming or updating a space doesn't always have to mean a large-scale renovation or big budget. Maybe you are looking for small ways to infuse that midcentury *feel* into your home without a big overhaul. In some cases, it could be as simple as swapping one material for another or finding just the right vintage retro clock to make your space more mid-mod. Mixing in MCM-inspired colors, patterns, textures, and treasured objects can take a space from just a room with four walls to an environment that evokes comfort and joy.

Throughout each chapter, you'll also find sidebars with helpful information and accessible tips and tricks:

NAMES TO KNOW: From midcentury modern icons to up-and-coming designers and manufacturers, I'll share vendors and artists to keep in mind for inspiration and products.

MIDCENTURY MODERN FOR TWENTY-FIRST-CENTURY FAMILIES: With a dog and two active kids, my household is hectic and often messy. Throughout the book I'll give some tips for adding MCM touches that can support real-life, everyday living.

DESIGN ON A BUDGET: Great design does not have to be expensive! From DIY to reuse, there are so many ways to achieve midcentury style while on a budget.

FAQS: Over the years, I've noticed that most clients have the same questions, so I've pulled together some that I get asked most often.

But before we begin our journey, let's take a quick detour through the basics of a typical MCM home and the fundamental building blocks of midcentury modern design. Every home needs a good foundation, after all.

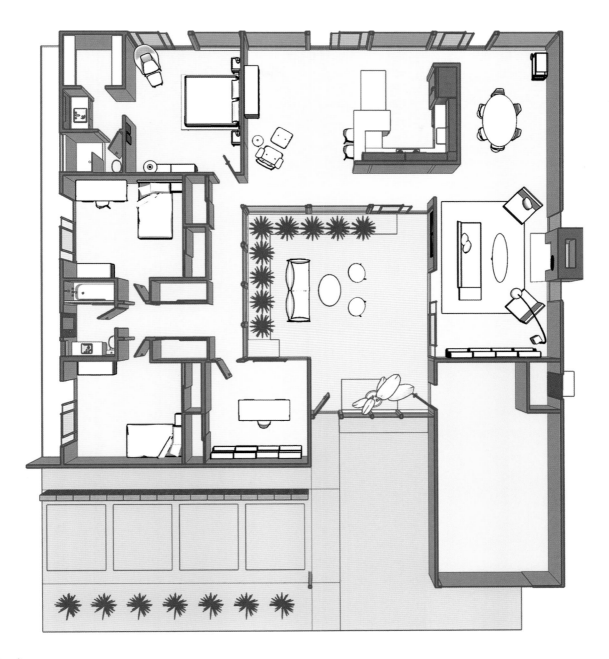

Anatomy of a Midcentury Modern Home

From unique entryways and courtyard atriums to formal living rooms, galley kitchens, modest-sized bedrooms, and everything in between, midcentury modern homes shared a variety of characteristics, no matter how the home was laid out.

THE EXTERIOR

Where I reside in the San Francisco Bay Area, there are a number of neighborhoods with modernist-style homes built during the 1950s to early 1970s. The neighborhood adjacent to mine features more traditional tract California ranch houses, built in a similar period but with markedly different exteriors. What makes them different? The MCM houses are single story with boxy and rectangular silhouettes and slim, angular, or flat rooflines; the ranch homes have front porches, window shutters, decorative trim work around the roofline, and more traditional house rooflines with shingled roofs, plus many with second stories. Basically, modernist-style homes lack the ranches' decorative elements and are more streamlined, almost plain in comparison.

MCM exteriors typically consist of thin wood siding or board and batten and are sometimes paired with just a touch of other materials, such as concrete masonry unit (CMU), stacked brick, or stone. There is often a sense of asymmetry to a midcentury modern home's exterior. You'll find a carport instead of a single- or double-car garage. Sometimes you'll see an interior courtyard or atrium, possibly surrounded by glass panels, which provide a view into the home's interior while also acting as an additional outdoor area.

In a handful of the home models in my neighborhood, there's not a single window facing out to the street. Instead, you first view the structure and shape of the house exterior, with maybe a transom or clerestory window to give hint to the details that are inside the home. I am personally drawn to that bit of mystery. What lies beyond the front door or courtyard? For those stepping into a midcentury modern home for the first time, there is usually a moment of surprise when they view the large expanse of glass often found inside these style homes. It's that aha moment that isn't initially revealed from the front entrance of the house.

Classic midcentury modern architecture was built upon post-and-beam construction, which allowed for the large spans of glass, commonly found in homes built during the period. Another signature feature was slightly angled or flat rooflines. The exterior shapes of the homes were usually not ornate but quite linear, boxy, and simple.

THE FAMILY AND LIVING ROOMS

Traditionally, midcentury modern living rooms and family rooms were designed for seating, family time, and entertaining. There might have been a television in a family room, but it certainly was not the focal point (nor were televisions sixty to seventy-five inches wide, like in the image above!). Instead, fireplaces, often built from brick or stone that matched the building's exterior, were a big (and functional) design feature, with the seating centered in front of it, the perfect spot for hanging out, reading a book, or playing a board game.

THE KITCHEN

Midcentury kitchens were designed for the task of cooking (specifically for one cook), not for multifunctionality and entertaining, like today's kitchens. A typical layout could include a straightforward galley shape with a cooktop, oven, sink, and cupboard storage. Sometimes there was a meager countertop workspace planned into the design, or a small peninsula might offer a bit of workspace while doubling as a place for kids to eat. Kitchen cabinetry was simple, with flat slab doors and drawers. There were no trim details on a cabinet front, no Shaker-style frames or fancy molding.

In many midcentury homes, including my Eichler home, the original cooktop was installed at a very low height. I stand a mighty 5'1" tall, so the height of the original cooktops and stoves are perfect for me, but I've had many taller clients complain about having to constantly bend over while cooking (and how they're always banging their heads on the original upper cabinets above a stove, which are also set low).

THE DINING ROOM

Dining rooms provided a central place for four to six people to sit for nightly family meals. An interesting light piece might have been the focal point above the dining table, with additional storage, such as a standalone credenza or sideboard, nearby.

The Saarinen dining table has become nearly synonymous with midcentury modern design. The pedestal-style base is a popular design for tables commonly found today, derived from Eero Saarinen's original vision. He wanted to solve the issue of the unsightly view of multiple legs underneath a table resulting from the traditional four-legged design of dining chairs and tables. His solution? A simple, sculptural metal base that allows for multiple chairs to gather around a table without the extraneous legs. This design evolved into an entire collection, which included Tulip chairs and stools and a variety of tabletop sizes, all with customizable tops and upholstery choices.

THE BEDROOMS

Bedroom spaces typically accommodated a bed, a nightstand or two, and a dresser. In the children's rooms, there may have also been space for a desk. The bedroom areas were designed for rest, so typically, the rooms were not made to accommodate extraneous furniture or seating. They certainly weren't designed for tons of kids' toys, gaming systems, and computer stations!

THE BATHROOM

Bathrooms were planned solely for their most basic functions. Midcentury bathrooms were often tiled floor to ceiling, sometimes in monochromatic colors (think pink and baby blue!), with even the sinks and toilets to match, like the one featured on page 174. Oftentimes, only the guest or kids' bathrooms had a bathtub, and the primary bathroom had a very small step-in or enclosed shower.

This teenager's bathroom was inspired by a love of Palm Springs, mecca of all things midcentury modern. We took the room from a traditional ranch-style space to completely MCM by adding a wallpaper patterned with palm trees and mid-mod architecture, pink tile, and a terrazzo-inspired quartz countertop and backsplash.

FRANK LLOYD WRIGHT COLLECTED WRITINGS VOLUME 7 1795–1985

FRANK LLOYD WRIGHT
DESIGNS FOR AN AMERICAN LANDSCAPE 1922–1932   DAVID G. DE LONG   ABRAMS

FRANK LLOYD WRIGHT
ARCHITECT

Key Elements of Midcentury Modern Design

Now that you have a good sense of the basic floor plan of a midcentury modern home, let's explore the specific features, elements, and characteristics of midcentury modern design. All the design guideposts and considerations to come build on the ideas discussed in this section, so you might want to place a bookmark here for easy reference later.

Whether you live in an apartment, condo, loft, modern house, midcentury modern house, or something in between, there are many wonderful aspects of midcentury design that can be brought into any space. MCM-inspired design offers a unique simplicity, functionality, and an aesthetically pleasing visual design, which can bring interest to your home—no matter what your primary style may be.

ART AND DESIGN PRINCIPLES

Midcentury modern artwork includes a variety of mediums and styles, but a few key themes include abstract art, geometric patterns, sculptural and organic shapes, and influences from the Bauhaus movement, which centered around the principle of form following function.

COLOR PALETTES

Color palettes ranged from bright pops of primary colors like red, blue, and yellow to groovy shades of turquoise, chartreuse, orange, and brown to pastel palettes including light pink, pale yellow, baby blue, and sea green. On the right are a few example palettes of how colors work together to give a midcentury feel.

During the midcentury era, designers hailing from all around the world were creating innovative furniture and designs. This included Charles and Ray Eames and Isamu Noguchi in the United States, Danish designers Hans Wegner and Arne Jacobsen, and Italian architect and designer Gio Ponti. Designs produced during this period share common design principles but are filtered through the nuances of different cultures and the blend of design materials that were available to them at the time.

There are many important artists who made a name for themselves, from furniture designers to photographers and ceramicists. Many contemporary artists, like Jonathan Adler and Shag, produce new artwork and design pieces inspired by the artists and themes of this period with a fresh perspective. Here are a number of artists whose work has influenced the midcentury modern movement and continues to inspire creatives and design enthusiasts today.

Slim Aarons (photography)
Ruth Asawa (wire sculpture, public commissions)
Alexander Calder (wire sculpture, mobiles, outdoor works/public commissions)
Charles Eames (furniture, toys, home accessories)
Ray Eames (graphic design, textiles)
Alexander Girard (architecture, interior design, furniture, industrial design, textiles)
Edith Heath (pottery, stoneware, dinnerware)
Ellsworth Kelly (painting, drawing, sculpture)
Jackson Pollock (painting)
Isamu Noguchi (sculpture, furniture, lighting, architecture, landscaping)
Mark Rothko (painting)

SHAPES AND PATTERNS

Midcentury modern art included a lot of lines and geometric shapes. Triangles, hexagons, squares, circles, and half-moons were often repeated or combined to create a larger patterns and designs. A line combined with simple circles could all of a sudden become a more intricate, unique pattern. Designers like Ray Eames and Alexander Girard created patterns that are the signature of midcentury modern graphic and textile design and provide inspiration to new designs today.

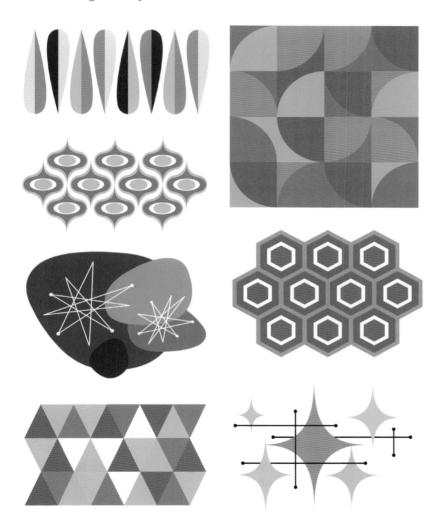

When looking for pieces of art to add to your home, remember to look beyond wall art. Plenty of pottery, ceramics, and stone and metal sculptures all have MCM design origins and can add wonderful interest to a space, such as this ceramics collection.

MIDCENTURY MODERN MATERIALS

Although midcentury modern homes varied in size, shape, and layout, they shared a subset of similar building materials—often what was readily available at the time. As such, a mix of components was common: stone or wood flooring, brick or metal fireplaces, laminate and chrome finishes in kitchens and bathrooms, and so on.

WOOD

Deep, warm woods such as teak, walnut, and rosewood were popular choices for MCM designers. Teak and walnut tend to come in warm brown tones, with rosewood bringing in a deep red-brown. Much of midcentury modern furniture is rooted in Danish design; the Danes initially utilized teak in their furniture, sourcing what was similar to American black cherry, in following of American Shaker furniture.

These warm colors really help define a room and envelop it in rich color and texture. Wood was used for everything from furniture to interior and exterior wall paneling. Bending and molding plywood into furniture was a brand-new concept at the time, allowing designers to make interesting shapes. The use of bent plywood paved the way for pieces to be both functional and beautiful. Plywood comes in lighter, almost blond tones, which offered up a more modern look to furniture pieces or cabinetry that wasn't quite so dark.

Cork was another common wood material found in spaces from flooring to furniture design, which found new popularity after the iconic American architect Frank Lloyd Wright used cork as a flooring choice for his home designs, like in the photo at right.

OPPOSITE: The original wood paneling and stone entryway stand the test of time, bringing nature right inside the home.

METAL

Brass, polished chrome, and stainless steel were common metals used in a variety of areas and were found in everything from building facades and fireplaces to appliances, fixtures, and decor accents. Stainless steel was discovered in the early 1900s and by the 1930s through 1950s became the standard material used in everything from appliances to kitchen sinks.

A special feature of this custom midcentury home is an original fireplace, constructed with a matte black metal hood, concrete block facade, and floating aggregate hearth.

STONE

Flagstone, concrete, terrazzo, brick, slate, and marble were used as both building materials and finishing touches on furniture like dining or coffee tables. Stonework often used locally sourced materials, such as granite or flagstone. The use of stone helped drive the idea of bringing nature inside, a primary theme of modernist design. Concrete breeze-blocks with intricate patterns were also used for building facades and decorative fences due to its lower cost than other common materials like brick.

TILE

In addition to the traditional use of tile in bathrooms and kitchens, it was sometimes featured on the outside of houses as a design element. Tile was created in many geometric shapes, including squares, rectangles, triangles, and hexagons, and made in a variety of materials, including glass, porcelain, and clay.

SYNTHETIC MATERIALS

Engineered materials like plastics, melamine, resin, vinyl, and fiberglass were all commonly used to craft everything from plates to chairs to flooring. The ease with which they could be bent and manipulated allowed the creation of sculptural pieces, such as molded fiberglass dining chairs.

There are a few ways to install tile, including straight set and offset. Straight set tiles are installed right next to and on top of one another. This installation was a very common in midcentury modern designs and its clean lines work well in nearly any use, whether for floor tile, bathtub or shower tile, or kitchen backsplashes. In an offset installation, there is a staggered pattern. One tile can be installed halfway into or over the next tile or one third of a way into the next tile, for a repeating, stepped pattern.

The flooring material you choose can totally change the feel of a space and help different rooms feel cohesive. Below are some of the most common MCM flooring materials and some substitutes you can use instead to get the same look with modern durability.

Original Flooring Materials	New Substitutes for Original Material
Terrazzo	Newly poured terrazzo or terrazzo-look porcelain tile
Concrete	Newly poured concrete, repolished concrete, or concrete-look porcelain tile in a large format for a more seamless look
Cork	New cork (usually comes in floating click-together planks)
Hardwood flooring	Refinish original floors or new hardwood or engineered hardwood flooring
Slate/stonework/ flagstone	Porcelain tile that emulates slate can give the look of stone, but provide easier cleaning and maintenance

TEXTILES AND UPHOLSTERY

Designed to be functional and fashionable, midcentury modern textiles and upholstery were known for their fun patterns and great textures. Materials like wool, linen, velvet, chenille, and bouclé were used in curtains, pillows, and furniture. Leather was also combined with other materials to give furniture a soft feel despite the hard surfaces. Another way to bring in natural materials was the use of grass cloth, which added a tactile and soft texture to the space.

FURNITURE

The key features of midcentury modern furniture are simplicity, functionality, and form. Much midcentury modern furniture was originally crafted in Scandinavian countries such as Denmark, and these designs influenced artists and designers from all over the world. MCM furniture was smaller in scale, designed with simplicity and function in mind—plus it had to be sized to fit in the more modest rooms.

SEATING

Sofas: Instead of oversized sectionals that seated ten, big roll-arm styles on the sofa ends, and overstuffed cushions, MCM sofas usually had clean, simple corners. More realistically, a petite loveseat and a matching set of sleek lounge chairs might have been found in a living room, arranged around a small coffee table and some matching side tables. Sofas usually had a two- or three-cushion seat base with curved designs that integrated the sofa shape, cushions, and upholstery for a one-piece look. They had petite legs, cushioned seats and backs, and linear (not overly rounded) arm shapes.

WHAT MAKES A SOFA MIDCENTURY MODERN?

A sofa can be from the midcentury (from the 1930s to 1960s) but not necessarily midcentury modern in style. Midcentury modern sofas tended to have clean, modern lines, simple tapered legs (wood or metal) and straight arms. Not all furniture designed and made in this era share these traits. I frequent estate sales and see a lot of furniture from the 1940s and 1950s that have more curved lines and ornate design. While beautiful, these sofas are very different from the modernist styles of the time and wouldn't be considered "midcentury modern."

Chairs and ottomans: Some midcentury lounge chairs mimicked sofa styles with wood frames, webbed seating, and corresponding seat and back cushions. Sculptural chairs, such as the Womb chair (as seen on the Table of Contents), offered comfortable seating while also providing beautiful color, shape, and texture to a room. Metal chairs took on a whole new look, with futuristic shapes, such as the Bertoia wire chair (similar to those on pages 198 and 201). Breakthroughs in technology and manufacturing allowed for chairs to be mass produced from materials like fiberglass and plastic, which were revolutionary for their time but are now very common today.

Stools: The difference between a counter stool and a barstool is the height of the seat. A barstool is a few inches higher, which works well for kitchens that have a higher counter height. Look for clean lines and simple shapes made from molded plastic, fiberglass, metal, and wood, or a combination of all of these materials, to recreate a midcentury look.

Benches: Classic bench designs included slatted wood benches and teak or walnut benches with an upholstered cushion seat. They had hairpin or simple legs.

Iconic midcentury modern design was pioneered by some of the greats, including power design couple Charles and Ray Eames and Herman Miller. When looking for newly manufactured midcentury-inspired furniture designs, look for similar design details, such as particular finishes, and pay attention to the furniture size and scale.

Harry Bertoia
Anna Castelli Ferrieri
Norman Cherner
Charles and Ray Eames
Eileen Gray
Arne Jacobsen
Florence Knoll
Greta Magnusson-
  Grossman
Herman Miller
George Nelson
Charlotte Perriand
Louis Poulsen
Eero Saarinen
Hans Wegner
Eva Zeisel

TABLES AND DESKS

Coffee tables: Midcentury coffee tables were petite to match the scale of loveseats or sofas. They typically came in surfboard, oval, boomerang, and circular shapes, with tapered or hairpin legs. Some designs featured nestled tables that could double as a larger or longer coffee table or be split up into side tables.

Side tables: In general, side tables were bought for functionality and were not overly ornate. There are some iconic midcentury modern designs that feature a tulip shape or a metal spindle-style base. Other styles include nesting tables, or a group of tables of varying sizes and heights that can be used together or separately. Nesting tables ranged from simple cube and rectangular shapes to groups of boomerangs and ovals.

Dining tables: There are a few standard midcentury dining table shapes that can work for a number of functional needs yet also imbue a room with a mid-mod style. Traditionally MCM tables were simple and straightforward. Rectangular tables had four legs; round and oval tables sometimes had a single pedestal. Tabletops were crafted from stone, such as marble, walnut, or laminate. Many classic midcentury modern designers and manufacturers offered tables with additional or integrated leaves, which allowed them to go from seating four to ten or more guests. All designs were created to make the tables unobtrusive in the space.

Desks: Steel and wood were common materials for office desks, which were functional and simple, without ornate details: a simple tabletop with legs and perhaps a few drawers for storage to keep things tidy in the office area.

BEDS, DRESSERS, AND NIGHTSTANDS

Bedframes and headboards: Simplicity is what ties together the design of a classic midcentury modern bedroom set. They are usually made from wood, such as walnut, with a simple headboard or could include an upholstered fabric headboard.

Dressers: Typically, midcentury dressers were made from walnut, teak, or rosewood. Not overly ornate, they were sleek and functional. Drawers might have had the cabinet pulls designed right into the piece, so there was no need for additional hardware. Dressers often came with a matching mirror, either mounted to the top of the dresser or to be hung above.

Nightstands: Original midcentury modern bedroom furniture could include integrated nightstands, which were already built into a bedframe for an all-in-one bedroom set. Petite legs held up a simple design, usually consisting of one- or two-drawer storage.

BOOKCASES, SHELVING, AND STORAGE

Bookcases and shelving: Shelving was typically mounted to the wall to give it the illusion of floating. It offered a lot of storage, but the lack of legs meant it didn't feel overwhelming in a space. From standard cubby-style to a mix of metal rods and shelves, known as a "string system," the design was always minimalist. Freestanding bookcases and étagères stood on simple hairpin or tapered legs and would sometimes mix open display shelves with sliding doors.

Sideboards and credenzas: Wooden sideboards and credenzas were simple in design yet served multiple functions. They provided storage for things like glassware and silverware and doubled as serving areas when entertaining guests. Sliding doors allowed for closed storage without the need to swing cabinet doors open.

Bar carts: Midcentury bar carts were made from materials such as walnut or teak, with metal accents such as brass.

APPLIANCES

Stainless-steel finishes were commonplace for appliances. In later years, appliances in bright colors such as yellow, orange, and blue dominated kitchen designs.

Media storage wasn't as necessary as it is today, but a freestanding unit with a record player, a radio, and record storage was commonly found in homes during the midcentury.

LIGHTING

Many traditional light fixtures offered a futuristic feel to match the worldwide fascination with space and technology. Midcentury-inspired lighting in particular featured a variety of sparkly finishes such as chrome and brass, which can contribute to that final layer of polish in a room design. The right lighting can be functional while still doubling as a cool art piece to look at when the fixture is not in use. Some of the most iconic fixtures and shapes included:

Sputniks or atomic style: The Space Race was pervasive during the midcentury, even influencing home decor and fashion trends—hence products that had futuristic, space-related design.

Globes and bubbles: Globes were the go-to lighting shape for midcentury houses. They could be found everywhere, from the front entry to hallways to kitchens and bathrooms. Like globes, bubble-shaped lighting was all the rage during the midcentury, and could be found as multiple clusters in chandeliers or a single orb as a pendant light. Other classic table lamp designs featured bulbous mushroom-style shapes.

WHERE SHOULD I USE DIFFERENT TYPES OF LIGHTING?

From increasing functionality to bringing visual interest, the right type of lighting can make all the difference in a room.

Chandeliers: Usually ornate, chandeliers add visual interest. They're a great option when you want a showstopper moment, such as hanging in entryways, from high ceilings, over dining tables, or as a living room centerpiece.

Flush-mount lights: Light fixtures that mount directly to the ceiling work well in spaces where the ceiling is not very high. Flush-mount lighting is found in nearly any room, and is installed right against the ceiling. Lighting that has a small gap between the ceiling and the light fixture, typically a very short rod, are called semi-flush-mount, but they still fit the goal of not taking up too much vertical space.

Pendants: Similar to chandeliers, pendants work well over spaces that need functional lighting as well a bit of flair, such as a kitchen island. They typically aren't as wide as chandeliers but can still provide a unique design moment. Even bathrooms can feature pendants as an interesting, different way to add lighting and personality.

Sconces: Sconces are wall mounted and can direct light up, down, or sideways. They work in areas where you don't want to take up floor space since they float on a wall.

Table lamps: Table lamps come in all shapes and sizes and can solve all kinds of lighting needs. On top of a credenza or dresser, they can add interest or create mood lighting. On a bedside table, they can provide functional lighting.

Task lamps: Task lamps, such as floor or desk lamps, can be moved around to provide additional light. Some can be used to light a room in addition or instead of overhead lighting or be placed in specific areas.

The Arco Floor Lamp, designed by Achille Castiglioni and brother Pier Giacomo for the company FLOS Lighting, is probably one of the most classic mid-century lamps. It features a suspended globe pendant on a large, arching arm, which is attached to a slab of marble. It works well in rooms with high ceilings and was designed to evenly distribute light under the light source so that the user isn't blinded when sitting under the lamp shade.

2 CREATING A MIDCENTURY MODERN LIVING ROOM

I t doesn't matter if you live in a compact apartment, a full-size home, or something in between, there's nothing better than a living area that is both comfortable and functional—except maybe one that's also beautiful, right? Thankfully it's not hard to create a midcentury-inspired space fit for relaxing or entertaining.

Pick the Right Furniture and Floor Plan

After learning the hallmarks of midcentury modern furniture in chapter 1 (page 39), you've found the perfect pieces. Now what? When it comes to designing a living room, one of the most-asked questions we get is: *Where do I put the sofa?* Furniture placement can be really tricky, and if it's not quite right, it can have a big effect on the overall feel of your room. Here are some simple guidelines to help.

Think about how you'll use the space. Living rooms can serve a several purposes. In some homes, it's the primary lounging and hanging-out space. Or perhaps you have a separate area for more casual relaxing and the living area is reserved for more formal entertaining or hosting. Figuring out how you'd like the space to function is an important step, which allows you to plan the furniture placement with that goal in mind. I've provided three potential layouts below, with some explanation for each on the right.

Consider the flow. Every home has a different layout, so it's important to think about the typical flow of people throughout the space. You wouldn't want to position your furniture in a way that blocks an entrance or exit. Additionally, you'd want to avoid obstructing windows or other features and instead should orient the seating around them.

If you have an open floor plan, you'll want to take into account any adjacent spaces, too. Maybe your living room and dining space are shared. But if you don't want the television to become a distraction during mealtime, you'll want to pay attention to where you place it. Or perhaps the living room is also a work-from-home area (more on office spaces on page 100). You'll want to make sure you position your furniture so that each designated function has enough space.

1

HOW SHOULD I POSITION MY FURNITURE?

Here are a few examples of different ways to layout your living room, depending on how you plan to use the space.

1 Relaxation these days often includes curling up on the couch to watch your favorite show or a movie. If that's how your family will primarily use the space, placing the TV in a place of prominence with a sofa positioned directly in front of it is the way to go. If you don't have room for a sofa plus a separate chair, an L-shaped sectional can give you more seating room while not taking up a wider area. Sometimes we angle a comfy lounge chair (or two) toward the television, with a sofa placed adjacent. This orientation is definitely a bonus for whoever is lucky enough to sit in the lounge chair!

2 If you're big on entertaining and plan to use your living room for social gatherings, try pairing a sofa with two adjacent chairs or have two sofas facing each other to allow for conversations to flow. For those with kids or anyone who enjoys a game night, it can be a great way to orient the seating around a central coffee table for playing board games. Having a nearby bench or some floor cushions are more ways to bring in comfy added seating when needed, that can be tucked away when not in use.

3 Perhaps you don't have a television in a main room or you prefer to not have it be the primary focus of the space. You'll want to pick a different focal point—maybe you're lucky enough to have a show-stopping fireplace or a gorgeous view. If so, you can orient the main seating to face this feature. When possible, a sofa should be symmetrical to the main point of interest, or at least in a position with a close view. You can then anchor other pieces, like another side chair or two near the sofa, to balance out the rest of the space and help create a cohesive seating area.

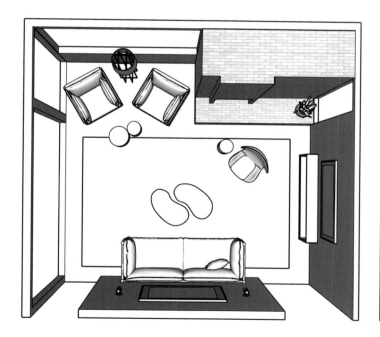

2

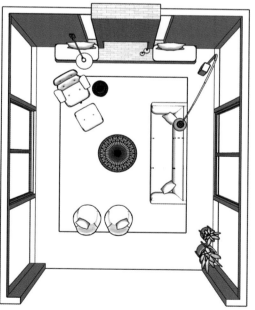

3

There's tons to consider when you shop for furniture. Do you like firm cushions or something softer? Are you tall or short? Do you have pets? Do you want to be able to curl up on your accent chair to read a book, or is it more for looks? Will it be able to withstand your kids' wrestling matches? Plus, there's the price tag, which makes it all the more important to take your time before making a purchase. So to help you out, here are some tips to make the process a bit easier.

Sit for yourself. When possible, we recommend clients visit a local retailer or showroom so they can try out the furniture pieces for themselves.

Read reviews. If you need to purchase online, it's important to read all the online reviews—especially the bad ones! You can usually get an idea of all potential issues from negative reviews.

Choose fabrics wisely. If you have kids or pets, opting for family-friendly, stain-resistant fabrics is key. Shop for upholstery fabrics that are labeled "performance," which can hold up to stains and daily wear and tear. Leather or vegan leather can also be a great option for busy or active households. Many retailers and websites allow you to try out samples first for different fabrics. This is a perfect way to bring a piece of the upholstery into your home so you can see how it feels and looks in your space and its lighting.

Measure more than once! There's nothing worse than finally getting a piece of furniture into your space only to find out it's an inch too wide for where you want it.

Utilize technology. A lot of websites now allow you to see what a piece of furniture would look like in your space, even in 3D. This can give a bit more insight into the details of a piece that flat photos won't show.

Knowledge is power. Whether you purchase in person or online, make sure you're familiar with the return policy, delivery specifics, and any warranties.

For their Eichler home, our clients in Los Altos, CA, found this vintage Adrian Pearsall sofa, which was given new cushions and reupholstered in a vibrant fabric to give it another generation of use.

A number of contemporary furniture retailers and furniture design companies offer modern pieces that fit in nicely when combined with the more classic midcentury modern style. A modern MCM piece tends to have simple legs, isn't fussy, and is often made from just a few materials, such as wood, metal, or stone. All of these characteristics are rooted in midcentury modern design and are found at many shops and retailers like the ones listed here.

Some furniture retailers, such as Design Within Reach, carry only the originals or the new production of authentic, original designs. Other retailers, such as Blu Dot and Floyd, design their own unique new pieces, many of which are designed and made in the USA. When searching for the perfect pieces for our clients, we like pairing both original, authentic designs with newer modern pieces or vintage finds to put a unique twist on midcentury modern style.

Blu Dot
Casara Modern
Design Within Reach
Floyd
Gus* Modern
HAY
Room & Board
Scandinavian Designs
West Elm
World Market

Pets are an integral part of many families and households, but it can be hard to figure out how to strike a balance between having nice things and the havoc our furry friends can wreak. Thankfully, there are some ways to make sure your place is pet-proofed and still stylish.

Accessories: Bandanas are a great way to bring in some midcentury flair with inspired textiles. Leashes in bright colors can coordinate with your entryway color palette and hang from a classic Eames Hang-It-All hook set. (See page 180.)

Beds: Just like with beds for humans, there are many fabulous midcentury modern bed designs for pets! Look for wood bases with upholstered cushions or cushion beds made from geometric fabrics.

Washable or waterproof rugs: One of the first things we discovered after adopting our rescue dog, Velvet, shown here living her best life, is the need for washable rugs! Since then, rugs made from recycled materials have been our new favorite household item. These rugs can either be hosed down or put in the washing machine, depending on the brand and design, and many come in midcentury-inspired designs.

Feeding station: Find a dedicated spot to feed your pets, whether it's a corner that's of the way or a built-in feeding area. (Utilizing the toe-kick area underneath a kitchen cabinet is a great way to do this). Look for bowls that have simple shapes or lines. There are many great midcentury-inspired feeding stations that have wooden, mid-mod bases to house the water and food bowls.

Look for fabrics that are pet-friendly and stain resistant (more on that on page 55). Woven, textured fabrics can be a tad more forgiving to wear, tear, and stains. Cushion covers that can be removed and thrown into the washing machine are a lifesaver!

Window Treatments and Lighting Considerations

During the 1950s and 1960s, floor-to-ceiling curtains were often installed as window treatments, for both privacy and for decor. And while I do love the statement they can make, they often require custom lengths, the prices of which add up quickly. For this reason, we often choose to channel the midcentury modern idea of simplicity and functionality when it comes window treatments. Roller shades or cellular shades are a great pick. They provide privacy when closed (without covering up anything more than the glass itself) and when open, it's as if they aren't even there. This allows the furniture and decor in the room provide the visual interest.

But you'll likely need more than just windows to light your living room—especially at night. Look to light fixtures and lamps to add some MCM pizazz. In my space, I went with one of the most tried-and-true midcentury modern pieces—a Sputnik-shaped ceiling light overhead, which works well with the other lighting in the open floor plan. A Sputnik light diffuses lighting outward, which can help brighten a large area with just one light fixture. I waited years for the perfect floor lamp and finally found a vintage oversized one at a nearby estate sale. Its large scale gives it a prominent place in the room, and the light it gives off is perfect for reading a book.

For a condo in Palo Alto, California, shown on the opposite page, we opted for a classic Nelson Cigar floor lamp. During the day, it acts as a sculptural piece. The rounded oval style forms a very organic shape and gives softness to the space, while its petite size doesn't overwhelm the compact room. At night, it provides soft, diffused light, thanks to the thin coat of resinous lacquer and layer of plastic that forms the lamp's shade. In this condo floor plan, the living area is adjacent to the homeowner's work-from-home desk. It was important to make the living area distinctly conducive to relaxing once the workday was done.

We placed a unique mushroom-shaped floor lamp (at right) in the corner a living room in Walnut Creek, California. The bright white geometric shape provides the perfect contrast to the room's deep, warm walnut paneling. The round shape of the lamp shade also mimics the rounded shapes of the nearby stacked side tables. I've found it's always nice to include some repeating themes when grouping different items together in a vignette.

In my open-concept living room, I chose a Sputnik-shaped ceiling light, which diffuses light outward and can help brighten a large area.

Incorporate Warm Woods

Original midcentury homes were filled with wood tones, from the walls to the furniture, in part because wood paneling was a popular and readily available wall material but also because many MCM designers loved the idea of bringing nature inside. Warm woods like walnut and oak made for a sleek, calming way to put this design principle into action, especially in the living areas. Warm-toned coffee tables, shelves, credenzas, and chairs and sofas with wooden accents are also great (and mobile) ways to achieve a similar feeling without overwhelming small spaces.

Recently, wood panels have experienced revived popularity. And although some may feel that they can contribute to a dated or dark look, if used as an accent—versus, say, wrapping an entire room in paneling—the effect can be both modern and timeless.

OPPOSITE: In our home, we use a vintage Eames Molded Plywood Folding Screen as both artwork and a functional privacy screen.

A more accessible way to bring the warmth of natural wood to your living room, like the original paneling in this image, is to opt for a slat wall instead of paneling. You can create gorgeous slat walls with individual slats or pre-made panels made to look like individual slats—or you can trick everyone with a realistic wood-panel or slat-wall wallpaper.

We work with many clients whose living rooms lack a midcentury feel. They have white or painted-drywall walls that lack warmth and coziness. To combat this, we often install new wood paneling with a technique called "book-matching," where the wood grain in each panel, which comes from a single tree, is matched up perfectly with the ones next to it. The result is a visual representation of a tree's history.

Our project in Stanford, California, shown on the opposite page, had decades-old original wood paneling that still looked fresh. They are largely responsible for the warm, inviting feel of the living rooms, despite the very spacious area.

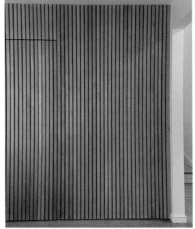

In many original midcentury houses,

the fireplace was the main focal point of a room. If you're lucky enough to have one in your space, here are some ways to restore, refurbish, or re-create without breaking the bank.

Original fireplaces were built with a variety of materials, ranging from brick to CMU to stone and metal. Fireplaces are not only functional, but they also add a strong visual statement to a space. My fireplace build includes clear glass window sidelights that frame the fireplace, so when one looks outside from inside the house, they can see the fireplace material extend out of the house. It's these details that make a midcentury home unique, which is why I try so hard to restore them when possible.

Older fireplace facades can sometimes be saved with surface cleaning or restoration. In our home and for several clients, we used a "soda blasting" treatment to clean up the brick or stone (or in our case, remove tile mortar that had been adhered to the original brick facade when a layer of limestone was applied over it).

If it is not possible to remove layers of add-ons, we can create a midcentury-inspired fireplace from scratch by bringing in period-appropriate materials. Several tile manufacturers offer a thin brick product that can be installed just like tile would but offers a brick-facade look. Thin brick is an affordable way to create a brick fireplace without actually re-laying bricks. Dimensional tile can also add texture to a fireplace while providing a strong visual moment. Lastly, if the original state of your fireplace is *really* not your vibe, paint can be a very budget-friendly way to bring new color into a space.

In this Eichler home, the original fireplace had been covered in different materials over the years. It wasn't feasible to get back to the original redbrick (seen through the windows) so we opted to install new, thin brick in a charcoal glaze to not only give a nod to the midcentury era but also give the fireplace a modern look.

Make It Pop

For every wood-paneled living space, there is a fun, bright alternative. For example, in a home in San Jose, California, we opted for bright white walls in the formal living room, which provide space to display the homeowner's icon-inspired DIY artwork. Many of the other spaces in the house have a bold feature moment, from a deep-blue fireplace to walnut accent walls, so we wanted this area to give some balance. The blank canvas of the white walls gives a gallery feel and makes it easy to switch out artwork when wanted. Instead of placing the usual sofa and chairs in this space, we opted for two sets of matching modern lounge chairs that were found on Craigslist. The homeowner enjoys hosting friends and family, and by placing the four chairs together we created the perfect spot to hang out during a dinner party.

A living space in Phoenix, Arizona (page 74), reflects the homeowner's passion for collecting vintage artwork and furniture. The client and I frequent local vintage resellers in person and online together, and we're always keeping one eye open for our favorite resellers' latest finds. One such find was a vintage sofa that we reupholstered in new MCM-inspired fabric and paired with a live-edge coffee table. I love how this room showcases mixing and matching different design ideas: The main midcentury modern pieces are the sofa and artwork, whereas other items, like the pillows and the rug, pull from different styles to give the space an eclectic, comfortable look.

And if you like things a bit more understated, that's okay, too. The small living room area featured above serves multiple functions, including relaxation and a workspace. To ensure a cozy, calm place to kick back once the workday is finished, we chose a more neutral palette of grays, creams, and blues. Midcentury-inspired pops of color are subtle, with the use of graphic patterned pillows in chartreuse, greens, and pinks. When selecting the sofa for the homeowner, it was very important that it be very soft and comfortable, perfect for reading and taking naps. We also wanted to place the furniture so the view and balcony were unobstructed. Printed artwork from a big-box retailer sits in simple white frames, which proves that you don't need to spend a ton to have beautiful pieces on your walls. Look for larger-scale prints and then frame them to make a bigger visual statement, especially when wall space is limited.

OPPOSITE: If you don't have the budget for a whole redesign, a stack of mod-colored coffee table books (extra points if it's an MCM design coffee-table book!) and a warm wood or lacquer tray can be enough midcentury flair. Creating a vignette on a table or shelf is an affordable, low-commitment way to bring some fun to your living room.

How do you inject your living room

with MCM style without it feeling like an exhibit in a museum—or emptying your bank account? The answer is to practice moderation. For example, if your living room is small, all you'll really need to get the vibe across is an inspired sofa. For a bigger space you'll probably want to add a coffee table or maybe an Eames-inspired accent chair or a mushroom-shaped table lamp.

The key to mixing different decor styles is to make sure there is a balance. I like to make sure to showcase special heirlooms and memories. In clients' homes, I have helped frame a special family portrait or a child's masterpiece. Sprinkling these personalized touches throughout your home makes it unique and, more importantly, *yours*.

In my home, I'm always switching out my artwork. At any point in time, you might find modern screen prints from local craft fairs next to a painting one of my kids did in school next to a vintage painting I just found at a garage sale, still in its old, original frame. Instead of trying to match everything, it's actually the eclectic mix of materials, frames, textures, and decades that help make things feel cohesive.

Not everyone (myself included!) has the budget to invest in gallery pieces. Much of the artwork in my home was sourced from local estate sales, antiques markets, garage sales. I especially love pieces with no signature. Maybe it was painted by the original homeowner? Maybe it was also found at a flea market. Perhaps it was painted by a family member or friend. The many stories a piece can hold fascinates me, and even though it's not worth money, it's likely one of a kind.

3

CREATING A MIDCENTURY MODERN
BEDROOM AND OFFICE SPACE

Your bedroom should be a place to relax and recharge, but that doesn't mean it can't have personality and mid-mod inspiration. Thankfully, interior design has the wonderful power to evoke different feelings and moods. In addition to choosing the right furniture, something as simple as painting a wall a certain color, hanging artwork, or wrapping a room in a material or pattern can give a space an entirely different atmosphere.

In this chapter I'll explore ways to create different midcentury modern moods in your bedroom, as well as touch on creating an inspired office space (page 100), since sometimes—despite the whole "relax and recharge" thing—our bedrooms are also our offices.

Go Geometric

Midcentury modern design is all about geometric shapes—from circles and half-moons to squares and beyond. (See chapter 1 for more inspiration!) Over the years, we've incorporated this idea into clients' bedrooms in a bunch of different ways.

To give a light, playful mood to a small bedroom in Walnut Creek, California, we wallpapered two walls with a modern pattern featuring repeating circles. The monochromatic green colorway adds vibrancy, but we kept the adjacent walls a bright white to give the eyes a space to rest. To add texture and a bit of softness to the room, we chose a velvet pouf and a hide rug. The round pouf keeps with the circle motif and provides additional casual seating. Throw pillows in various textures, colors, and patterns help bring the whole room together, and even the storage basket echoes the circles found throughout the space. If you are wary of introducing color to a space, getting adventurous with pillows or bedding is a great, low-stakes place to start!

For a mid-mod-inspired nursery, we opted for wallpaper with a graphic black-and-white pattern so the decor can easily change as the child grows. The walnut crib with classic MCM features is a great investment piece since it can convert to a toddler bed when needed. For more ideas for children's rooms, see page 88.

This small bedroom serves multiple functions. It's a guest bedroom as well as a video-gaming room, so we sourced a simple walnut twin bed frame that doubles as a sofa. The mix of bold colors and the geometric wallpaper immediately signals midcentury modern. If you don't want to mess with wallpaper, you can achieve a similar style with an MCM-inspired paint color and rely on your accessories like throw pillows to provide a geometric pop.

In this same home's guest bedroom, we anchored the room by wallpapering the biggest wall with a geometric black-and-white wallpaper. A black-and-white pattern can act almost as a neutral, which means you can use a wider variety of colors throughout the room or just take a subtle approach with a limited palette.

To let the wallpaper be the star of the show, we purposefully didn't hang up any artwork and chose a solid-color quilt and understated, sleek midcentury modern furniture.

Contemporary designers are creating new takes on wallpaper designs and patterns. These wallpaper designers offer fun, graphic designs and different textures that can help bring in that midcentury feel into a modern-day space. Peel-and-stick wallpaper is a fantastic way to achieve pattern and texture, without the full-time commitment of traditional pasted wallpaper.

Chasing Paper
Hygge & West
Habita
Maharam
Phillip Jeffries
Thatcher
Simple Stick Wallpaper by
  ABC Modern
Spoonflower (You can design your own!)

A vintage, geometric tension-pole lamp, which came from a neighbor's original MCM home, almost disappears into the space. It's multifunctional—storage plus lighting—and doesn't take up a ton of space, which also helps keep the room from looking too busy.

MID-CENTURY MODERN

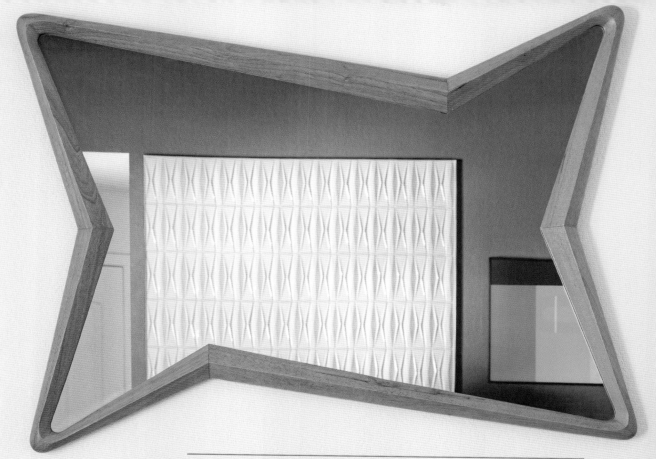

Midcentury modern design is also about being funky and fun! Even just a few key accessories can really make a bedroom exude that mid-mod cool. Here, a boomerang-style vintage mirror, a few graphic black-and-white pillows, and a vibrant Liza Minelli needlepoint pillow help bring a bed from plain to midcentury inspired. Neutral bedding is perfect backdrop to play with different colors and textures.

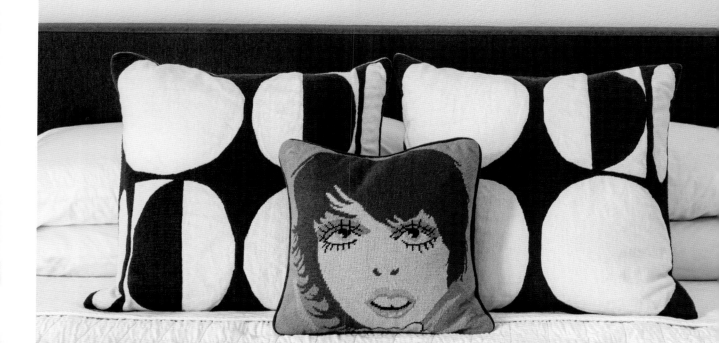

If a wall or two of pattern feels like overload, you can incorporate mid-mod geometry in more subdued ways. Our clients in Phoenix, Arizona, wanted their primary bedroom to be the ultimate relaxation zone and respite from busy, everyday family life while still oozing MCM charm. To accomplish this, we opted for calm white walls and kept the furniture and bedding inspired yet serene and simple.

To give the room texture, we chose a bedframe upholstered in a soothing blue and a woven rug in a natural fiber. To provide the graphic elements, we looked to a large painting with monochromatic yellow shapes and curtains with a complementary color and design. The warmer colors of the accents and the wooden furniture play off the blue of the bedframe to create a warm, relaxing space. The different textures and colors help make the room feel cozy and comfortable, so don't be afraid to experiment, especially when you're keeping things relatively unassuming.

If all-over wallpaper is out of the budget, or being surrounded by pattern gives you anxiety, try framing a wallpaper sample and hanging it on the wall instead. Or you could pick three coordinating patterns and create a triptych!

You can also make your own "wallpaper" with paint! I was inspired by the graphic design on the cover of a coffee table book about the iconic midcentury designers Charles and Ray Eames, so I decided to take a cut a piece of cardboard into a triangle and use it as a stencil to create a repeating pattern on the wall. I repurposed leftover paints from another house project and, all of sudden, I had my own custom mural. For less mess, there are many great decals that will achieve the same look.

While having children comes with a

lot of kids' stuff, particularly in their bedrooms, there are many ways to create a more minimal midcentury modern style while still creating a fun, playful space for kids to rest and grow. If you would like to bring in the spirit of midcentury aesthetics into kids' bedrooms, here are a few tips to follow.

Look for dual- or multipurpose furniture. A timeless midcentury material is walnut, and there are many fantastic midcentury-inspired children's lines with walnut finishes, simple cone legs, and minimal lines. Many infant cribs transition to a toddler bed, then a twin bed, eliminating the need to buy new furniture sets every few years as a child grows.

Take advantage of vertical space. Even in a small room, you can maximize the space from floor to ceiling with the use of furniture pieces like bunkbeds, floating shelves, or wall-mounted storage. Many bunk beds offer a variety of functions on the floor or lower-level bunk, such as an extra bed, a study area, a dresser, or a play space. Choose models that are simple, without a lot of ornate bells and whistles, to maintain a modern feel.

Don't complicate the color palette. Look for furniture that is natural birch or walnut, or that is painted white or other midcentury colors, which will give a good base to build upon with accents and other decor. You can also try monochromatic tones or black and white or gray, which will allow you to easily swap in different accent colors as your kids' interests and tastes change.

Pick resilient fabrics. When selecting upholstery material for items like beds or chairs, look for performance fabrics, which are designed for stain resistance and wear and tear. MCM-inspired color palettes and patterns can give a distinct look to kids' rooms, while still feeling age appropriate. Look for simple, repetitive patterns like circles, triangles, squares, or gridded lines. For rugs, try ones made from recycled materials, such as plastic bottles, or washable rugs. Some new recycled rugs can be hosed down outside or washed.

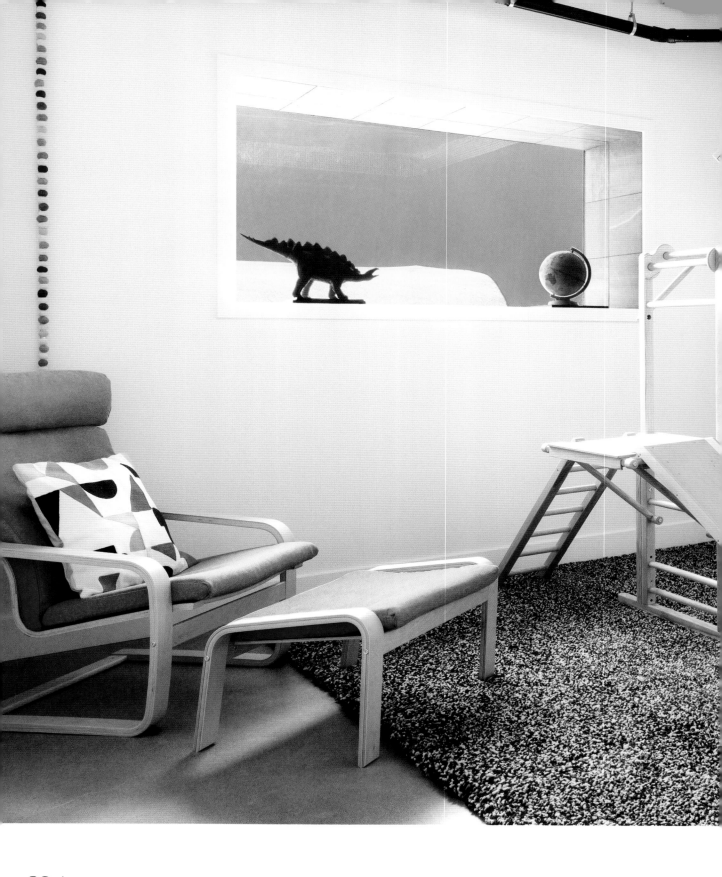

While this kids' playroom is designed for maximum fun, we also wanted it to feel at home with the rest of the historic midcentury-era home. The minimalist design of the chair, playset, and lounge area combined with the bright, graphic colors and geometric motifs all give off a modern feel. (Oh, and that blue expanse out the window? That's the family's swimming pool!)

Let Nature Inspire You

In today's busy world, it's especially important for a bedroom to feel relaxing and calm. Since midcentury modern design is rooted in nature, adding the touches of the outdoors to your space is a great way to imbue both serenity and mid-mod inspiration.

Our clients in Vermont are incredibly lucky to have a gorgeous view of a grassy meadow through their bedroom window. We wanted to let the natural views do the talking, so we made sure the decor complemented—not detracted from—the beauty. The simple bedframe is upholstered in a deep green and paired with an abstract rug in similar tones. The busyness of the rug adds visual interest, but the muted colors keep it from feeling garish. Its design is also mimicked in the neutral-toned artwork above the bed. The white bedding is light and airy and keeps the space from feeling too dark, but you'll notice it's decidedly not midcentury modern. We wanted to allow the room to reflect the clients' personalities, and we opted for a fun printed duvet that's still understated enough to blend in with the rest of the decor. The traditional midcentury wood-slat bench and bedside tables signal to the era, and work well with the gorgeous, rustic tongue-and-groove ceilings.

When it came time to decorate a bedroom in my house that was just big enough for a queen bed and two petite nightstands (page 94), I took inspiration from a duvet cover I loved, which featured an allover print derived from a mid-mod leaf pattern. From there, I chose the simple headboard upholstered in a complementary color. Both the bedding and the headboard contrast nicely with the warm wood-paneled walls, and when viewed all together they evoke the great outdoors. Above the bed hangs a DIY textile piece I created with yarn and a tree branch. It adds textures, breaks up the expanse of the wall, and brings the nature theme full circle.

If you don't have quite as nice a view outside your window, you can bring the beauty of nature indoors with earth-toned textiles, like bedding or rugs, and invest in furniture that feels warm and rustic. A long piece of driftwood can make for a beautiful natural sculpture. Tall, dried grasses look great in a cylindrical vase, which can provide a sense of geometry. Air plants or a small "living plant wall" can also bring fresh greenery inside. And while plants are always good for the interior environment, not everyone has a green thumb, and that's okay! There are some beautiful faux options available these days that will give the same feel without having to worry about keeping plants alive.

Bedding sets can get pricey. Creating your own duvet cover is a fun and easy way to make your own special bedding with a midcentury modern feel. No sewing machine? No problem! One of the first DIY projects I did in my first apartment was create a duvet cover using fabric and iron-on tape to seal the sides. Look for fun vintage fabric from online marketplaces or antique fairs. If sewing's not your thing, find a local upholsterer or seamstress to do the technical work. The result? A one-of-a-kind duvet cover unique to you!

Looking for a unique headboard that doesn't break the bank? Upholstering one in midcentury modern colors or patterns is going to be much more cost-effective than buying something new—plus, you'll get to choose the exact fabric you want. There are many online tutorials showing how to upholster headboards. They usually require a headboard, batting material, fabric, and a staple gun. That's it!

If you're not as DIY inclined, you can create MCM-inspired "headboards" with paint, wallpaper, or artwork above your bed.

I used this midcentury-inspired duvet cover as the inspiration for the whole bedroom. If you are at a loss for where to start your bedroom design palette, try searching for a bedding pattern that you love and that makes you feel relaxed. From there, you can start to pull in either color or pattern from the bedding to create your own sanctuary.

Embrace Minimalism

Much of midcentury modern design is based on the idea of minimalism, so it's a great match for those who want to embrace the ethos, whether out of necessity due to small square footage or as just a way of life. Although the idea of minimalism can be applied to any home space, it works especially well in bedrooms, where rest and relaxation are paramount, and you can achieve a fuss-free design in a variety of ways.

Instead of relying on midcentury modern colors and patterns to signify the era, you'll want to look toward more basic ideas. When it comes to choosing bedroom furniture for clients who prefer a minimal aesthetic, we try to use furniture with the MCM attributes mentioned in chapter 1 (page 39). For one client with a bedroom with limited space, we chose a simple headboard that had nightstands cleverly designed into it, which removed the visual weight of the nightstands' legs. You can incorporate this idea by using

We chose cream-colored fabric for the bed to provide a soft contrast to the warmer walnut-paneled walls, and the sconces look pretty, even when they are off—like jewelry for the wall.

floating shelves instead of bookcases or choosing mid-mod wall-mounted sconces instead of a typical table lamp, like we did for clients in both San Jose and Walnut Creek.

Another surefire way to limit the busyness of a room is to choose a limited color palette. For the bedrooms in San Jose and Walnut Creek, we found that decorating the spaces in neutrals made them feel cohesive and calming. The lighter colors also work especially well to balance the wood-paneled walls and traditional midcentury modern furniture. If you choose to go with a neutral color scheme, make sure to include different textures and layer different tones to create a space that feels cozy, not clinical.

Neither room has big statement artwork or flashy decor, either. Instead, small details like a tufted headboard, brass hardware, plants, and framed pictures give the spaces a bit of oomph and prevent them from feeling dark and impersonal.

To make sure this space didn't feel too heavy with the walnut-paneled wall, we chose a color palette of light-colored neutrals. The nightstands are family heirlooms, and we brought the subtle detail of their recessed brass handles into the interior rim of the wall sconces. Mixing metals and woods give the room added depth.

Choose Just a Little MCM

While bedroom furniture is always one of the quickest ways to imbue a room with midcentury modern charm, I know that not everyone has the budget or desire to go that route. So when looking to decorate a bedroom space, you can just select piece or two to get the point across. I love mixing styles because it gives personality to a space. It's all about the right mix and match that makes a room distinctly yours.

For example, a bedroom for a client in San Jose, California, doesn't exactly shout "midcentury modern." The tufted upholstered headboard is ornate and the lamps are, too. But they're paired with a classic MCM alarm clock and vintage nightstands and a bright pop of yellow in the bedding. You can achieve a similar feel by picking a few inspired accents. They could be as simple as a mid-mod planter, a throw pillow with a graphic pattern, or an era-inspired table lamp.

The Modern Home Office

These days, a home office can be headquartered anywhere—the sofa, the bedroom, the kitchen table. Regardless of whether you have a separate room, if you want your office area to have a mid-century modern feel, bringing in just a few select pieces can help define the space and give it that MCM spirit.

As has been suggested before, installing wall-mounted or floating furniture can help free up the visual space below, providing a more minimal, MCM look. The principle applies here, too, especially since office furniture can serve many functions, from a desk area to additional storage. Vintage or vintage-inspired wall-mounted desks and display systems are a great way to achieve this clean look. As a bonus, the budget invested in multiuse furniture gives you the biggest bang for your buck.

Alternatives to wall-mounted furniture include wooden desks with conical legs and, in the spirit of originally designed MCM office furniture, desks with simple metal bases and a large wood or laminate top. Having a bookcase nearby gives you a spot for storing books or papers, as well as a chance to display a few favorite items to personalize the space and make yours. Including these touches will make your office a place you enjoy spending time in.

And don't forget about ergonomic office chairs, which will ensure proper support for you for those long virtual meetings. Some of the best office chairs are designed by the same manufacturers from the 1950s and 1960s, the height of combining form and function.

HOW DO I CARVE OUT A HOME OFFICE SPACE?

While there are many perks of working from home, it can also be challenging to figure out the best spot for your home office, especially if you're sharing the space with other household members or if space is at a premium. Even bedrooms can serve as both a resting space and an office space, which is all the more reason the room design should be planned to meet both functions. If your room needs to serve multiple purposes, remember to dedicate distinct zones that can fulfill your goals. Even in the smallest areas, rest and work can coexist if you're resourceful with the space at hand.

When your work-from-home area is in a shared functional space, whether it's the kitchen, dining room, or a bedroom, try to carve out a dedicated spot for a desk and chair. You can help define different zones in a shared space by using rugs, accent walls, and decor—anything that will set off or signal a shift in setting.

Positioning the desk with your back to a wall can be helpful, so that there is always a solid space behind you when on virtual calls. This will also limit the view of other people coming in and out of your space. That option isn't always possible, however, which is where having a moveable room divider or screen can be handy. You can put up the screen during "office hours," giving you privacy, and then fold it away when no longer in use. This also helps create boundaries between work and rest hours, which is much needed during today's constantly connected work world. Having storage for work files can also be helpful. It can be nice to put away work-related materials so that visually, you can enjoy home life without being reminded of work.

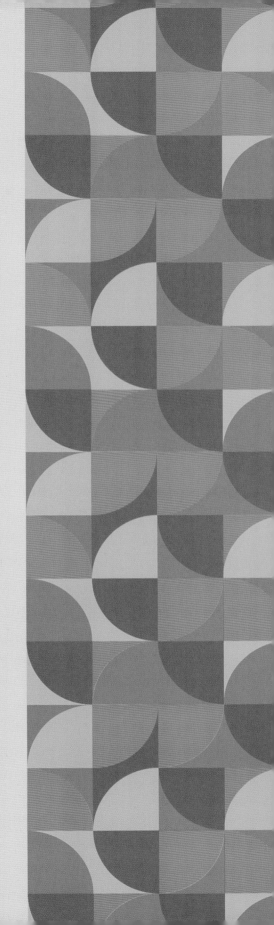

4 CREATING A MIDCENTURY MODERN
KITCHEN

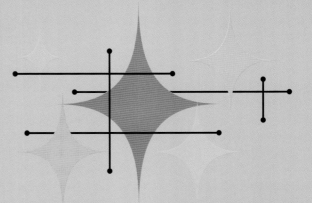

I've always found that the kitchen is the central heart of any home, so let's explore ways you can add a bit of midcentury flair to your space. When working with clients on a midcentury-inspired kitchen design, we try to strike a balance between incorporating similar materials from the era and making sure to keep modern-day functionality and practicality top of mind. However, even if you're not starting from scratch there are easy ways to add MCM-inspired touches to your kitchen.

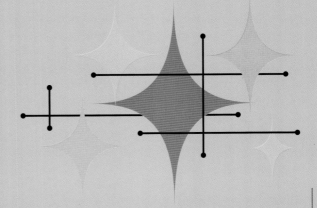

Consider Your Cabinets and Countertops

Two of the biggest features of any kitchen are the cabinets and countertops, so it's only natural that your design choices for both will have a big impact on the overall aesthetic. What you choose will define the "base layer" of the kitchen design and set the tone for the space.

CABINETS

Cabinet doors serve dual purposes. In addition to hiding all your stuff, they can give a kitchen a distinct personality. For a true midcentury modern look, the selection of period-appropriate cabinet style and finish is a key decision. Here are some design details to look for in kitchen cabinets that are particular to midcentury modern style:

Slab doors: Slab doors are flat and don't have any extra trim work the way Shaker-style cabinets do. The hardware is typically placed on the front corner or the middle; other times small notches or cutouts allow for a more minimal look.

Wood-finish doors: Warm woods like walnut and teak are solid MCM choices but can be expensive. For those on a budget, plywood and the inherent grain in the wood can offer a lighter yet still warm midcentury tone to a kitchen at a lower cost, and white oak can serve as a timeless finish for cabinets.

Painted or laminate doors: Midcentury modern kitchen cabinets originally came in painted wood. Today, painted wood cabinets or cabinets made from colored laminate are a great way to achieve the same look with added durability. You can bring in a favorite midcentury color, or you can go with gray or white to provide a neutral base for your kitchen design.

Bi-pass sliding doors: These doors slide horizontally instead of opening outward and were often found on credenzas and sideboards. They can give cabinets in small spaces functionality and a clean, modern look. They often had small notches or cutouts, which eliminated the need for additional hardware.

Built-in display boxes and storage: Small shelves and display boxes were used for storing things that could also serve as art objects, like cookbooks or dishware.

Reeded glass fronts: Reeded glass has a striped look. Glass allows a subtle peek at the items stored behind it for a cleaner, uncluttered look.

Ceiling-mounted cabinets: A classic midcentury cabinet design was to have them suspended from the ceiling by metal rods, like the ones on the opposite page. This gives an airiness to the space while also providing needed storage room.

Open shelving: Sometimes open shelving or display areas were specifically planned into a cabinet layout over areas such as windows, sinks, or cooktops, or at the end of a run of upper cabinets. These shelves often housed decorative items, knickknacks, and collectibles.

The bright, happy color palette of ochre, orange, light blue, and dark blue was inspired by colors on the cover of a coffee table book about design greats Charles and Ray Eames.

COUNTERTOPS

Countertops in midcentury homes were often made of laminate and sometimes stainless steel or even wood. Today, engineered quartz can emulate a wide variety of materials, such as terrazzo, concrete, and stone, and offer durability and longevity for everyday use and care. Since countertops can take up a large piece of the visual space in a room, what you choose is important: A lighter material, such as a white quartz with tiny flecks of stone, can add lightness and brightness to the space; wood or butcher-block countertops can add warmth; and darker-colored countertops can add depth or ground an area.

Countertops can also direct the eyes where to focus. A client had a kitchen with vibrant cabinets and a geometric tile backsplash, which we wanted to be the focal point of the room (page 115). To achieve this, we grounded the area with dark lower cabinets and used a lighter, almost white engineered-quartz material for the island, cooktop, and countertop. The effect is that the counter seems to disappear and allows the mint-green cabinets and intricate triangle-patterned backsplash to be the stars of the kitchen.

There are several companies that offer slab door and drawer fronts in real and manufactured wood veneers and laminates in fun midcentury hues. These products are designed to attach to IKEA-manufactured cabinet bases and allow you to go beyond the big-box retailer's offerings. This route can be a cost-friendly, DIY way to get a distinct mid-mod-inspired kitchen design.

THE SINK

Stainless steel and porcelain sinks were fairly common in midcentury homes and are still readily available today—you can even get them in fun colors. Many contemporary faucet designs are actually derived from those by architect and designer Arne Jacobsen for the Danish manufacturer VOLA, which was known for beautiful, clean shapes and lines. To channel midcentury modern through your faucets, stay away from overly ornate models with handle details or an oversized gooseneck style. Polished chrome is a traditional finish, but don't be afraid to install one in a bold color. (See page 160 for some inspiration.) If we all have to do dishes daily, why not make the chore more fun with a vibrant, midcentury-inspired faucet?

In a home in Phoenix, Arizona (at right), we installed a new vintage-inspired faucet and paired it with a classic white porcelain sink to provide an authentic mid-mod feel. This particular faucet was re-created from an original design from the 1940s and 1950s. The polished chrome base, retro handle levers, and iconic logo really pay homage to vintage kitchen design, so it looks like it is right out of a 1950s television advertisement or show.

Think of putting new hardware on old cabinets as you would adding jewelry to give new life to a favorite outfit. Search online resellers for vintage knobs and handles or try your luck at flea markets and thrift stores. Look for interesting midcentury inspired shapes, like bowties, half-moons, or mushroom knobs. Brass and polished chrome finishes are period-appropriate choices. If you can't find what you're looking for, you can also give your current hardware a facelift with some paint—I love the fun of bright-orange knobs on white cabinets!

If you're on a budget, think about refreshing existing cabinetry with a new coat of paint or wood refinishing, but be ready to roll up your sleeves! It involves quite a bit of labor to properly sand and prepare the cabinet surfaces so that the new paint will adhere to the cabinets.

Before you start picking out fun paint colors, you'll need to remove all doors and drawer fronts to allow for sanding, priming, and then several coats of cabinetry-specific paint, completed with a finish coat to protect the wood. Look for paint that is latex based or hybrid enamel, and don't forget a proper primer coat. A satin finish is one of my favorites to use on cabinetry because its mostly matte with a subtle shine that works well with the simple yet functional midcentury modern look.

If you want to preserve original materials and bring natural tones into your kitchen, refinishing wood cabinets can be great option—if they're made from natural woods like oak or maple and can still be sanded down to a fresh layer of wood. For cabinets with a wood veneer—a thin outer layer of wood glued to the cabinet substrate—it's probably not possible to sand down and refinish, so perhaps just primer and paint are your new friends!

Play with Pops of Color

Nothing says "midcentury modern" like a kitchen filled with pops of traditional color palettes of the era. Popular choices for this room include pastel blues, pinks, and yellows, as well as bolder tones such as orange, red, and turquoise. Bringing the outdoors inside is also a big principle of MCM design, so nature-derived colors like greens in shades of chartreuse and avocado and warm brown tones are great, too.

When selecting bright colors, try to balance them with the tones of the other materials in the space. For example, for a 1950s Eichler home kitchen design, we had the old cabinets repainted a mint green color to stay within the midcentury modern palette, and we paired them with a white tile backsplash and light concrete-look quartz countertops to freshen up the space. Including natural woods and darker colors can also keep the eyes from being overwhelmed by too many design elements competing for attention.

Perhaps a Pendant Light?

Pendant lighting over a kitchen island is the perfect way to add some midcentury sparkle—and sometimes color—to a kitchen. Look for atomic, cone, or bubble shapes. When selecting a pendant, consider the balance of your feature elements. If you want the pendant be the visual event of the kitchen, make sure the finishes and colors in the rest of the space don't compete with it. And if you have a bold design element, such as bright, intricate tile work, opt for functional lighting that leaves the tile as the star.

Have a Seat

If you have a kitchen island, selecting the right seating is an easy way to bring in a midcentury modern feel. Look for counter stools (or barstools, depending on your countertop height) that have H-shaped metal legs or tapered wood legs. You'll want a seat shape that's organic or slightly curved without an ornate seat back, which can look out of place with the rest of a minimal MCM kitchen. Bentwood, fiberglass, and meshed metal are all good options. If you'd like to add some color or texture, look for stools upholstered in traditional fabrics, or select a powder-coated metal.

With a generously sized island, it's important to select counter seating that is simple in style so you don't overwhelm the area. These low-back counter stools in a muted tone offer comfortable seating with a sleek profile, while the simple wood legs blend into the island. The globe pendants add functional lighting but are simple enough to not compete with the cabinetry and tile backsplash.

Backsplash Beauty

Perhaps you don't have the space for pendant lighting and new cabinets and countertops are out of the question. Don't worry! Backsplashes are one of the easiest ways to bring the midcentury into your modern kitchen. Best of all, redesigning a backsplash can accommodate all kinds of budgets and living situations.

When I was redesigning my kitchen, shown on page 122, I initially thought I wanted an orange cooking range to be the big visual moment, but the orange competed with the walnut cabinetry I'd picked out. Instead I chose a standard range and got creative with my backsplash. I settled on a beautiful turquoise tile in a diamond shape, which provided a nice contrast to the cabinetry. To mix things up a bit, I used the "Escher" pattern and white grout, which give the final backsplash a 3D look.

There are many levers you can pull to get that midcentury modern look in your kitchen backsplash. The first choice to make is a color. Muted tones, like pastels, can give visual interest without overwhelming the other elements in the room; peppy, active tones, like orange or turquoise, can make the backsplash the main event. If bright colors aren't for you, selecting a neutral tile color but installing it with a light gray grout can give the backsplash added dimension, and when installed stacked and not staggered, it's midcentury modern rooted.

Next, select a shape and figure out a pattern. Squares, rectangles, triangles, diamonds, and hexagons are all traditional MCM shapes. And since midcentury modern design was all about simplicity and clean lines, square or rectangular tile set on top of one another (versus staggered, like in a subway station) is a popular installation.

For a compact kitchen, we opted for a unique handcrafted tile in an Ogee Drop or fish-scale shape. The sea-inspired, blue-green color and scalloped shape provide a bold focal feature, which pairs well with simple white slab-door cabinetry. Since we didn't have a large expanse of backsplash to tile, the majority of the budget went toward the artisanal tile and was balanced with economical DIY-style kitchen cabinetry.

Do you want a new backsplash but can't or don't want to make a big tiling project out of it? There are peel-and-stick tile options, as well as tile decals that can make this project easy and affordable. If you don't need a waterproof area, patterned wallpaper can also make for a great backsplash-style background. Bring in midcentury colors, such as yellow or orange, or patterns with triangles or hexagons. Keep in mind, too, that you don't need to tile an entire wall to make a statement. Instead you can just focus on a small area, such as the area behind the range, which will still have an impact.

ABOVE: In this Palo Alto kitchen, the white cabinets let the fun back-splash sing. The custom colorway and special small-diamond tiles gave the kitchen a new feel without extensive renovations. The tile manufacturer has been active since 1950s, which was when the condo was built, so it was important for us to incorporate some original-style materials and colorways that the factory makes into the space.

RIGHT: Dimensional ceramic tile in an iconic 1950s oval pattern gives this backsplash texture. Each tile is made from an individual mold, making it a unique piece of art! We went to a local tilemaker's seconds warehouse and sourced the tile for a fraction of the original price. Sometimes there are small imperfections to seconds tile but when installed as a feature in a large amount of space, those details are not noticeable and to most, so it's well worth the cost savings!

For family-friendly dining seating, try fiberglass or plastic chairs or stools. They are highly durable, can be wiped down easily, and can be found in a variety of midcentury-inspired designs, such as the classic shell chair shape. Leather can also be a hardy upholstery for busy (and mess-prone) households.

Appliances Don't Have to Be Boring

Sometimes original appliances, like gas ranges, refrigerators, toasters, microwaves, and the iconic wall ovens, can be found in antiques stores or online, but the cost of refurbishing them can add up, and they won't offer modern energy efficiencies or any bells and whistles. Thankfully, there are now many companies that design retro replicas. One of these retro-feel appliances can really give your kitchen an air of authenticity. Plus, they're often offered in fun colors like orange and turquoise and can serve as decor in addition to being functional.

Remember Mid-Mod Accessories

A client's kitchen design isn't over until we add the finishing touches! Even if they're the only changes you make to your kitchen, these usually lower-budget items such as kitchen towels, soap dispensers, dishware, and storage can go a long way toward changing the vibe of the room. These items don't need to be vintage, but it's definitely fun to search for them! Here are some things to look for:

Patterns: Look for repeated geometric shapes like triangles, hexagons, diamonds, and crosses. Nature inspired a lot of midcentury modern design, so motifs of simple line drawings of flower petals, leaves, branches, and birds all speak to the time period.

Color: Complement or match your kitchen scheme, or use your kitchen accessories to introduce MCM colors such as orange, turquoise, yellow, pink, mint green, or aqua without going overboard. Even things like small dustpans come in midcentury colors these days.

Handcrafted feel: Handcrafted ceramics were popular in the 1960s and are experiencing a resurgence in home decor, from small artisans to big-box retailers. Look for organic shapes, a mix of materials, and speckles and imperfections, all details that make a piece feel authentic and can turn your everyday bowls, plates, and mugs into midcentury modern decor. Try a set of orange coffee mugs or some speckled robin's-egg-blue bowls—details reminiscent of original midcentury design.

Many contemporary appliance manufacturers offer the latest in cooking technology while also offering a plethora of vintage-inspired styles. Here are some of my favorites.

BlueStar
Smeg
Big Chill
AGA
Bertazzoni
Hestan
Galanz

Perhaps you have younger ones at home and breakable glass plates and drinkware aren't a good fit for this phase of your life. Bring in kid-friendly melamine dishware in midcentury-inspired colors or graphic patterns. Many of the modern-day tableware lines are inspired by the MCM greats such as Cathrineholm pieces.

WHAT SHOULD I LOOK FOR AT ESTATE SALES, FLEA MARKETS, AND THRIFT STORES?

Vintage dishware is an easy way to imbue a bit of MCM flair to your table settings. Plus, it feels good to give new life to items that otherwise might end up in landfill. Some well-known brands of the time were:

Cathrineholm: Catherineholm dishware, created in Norway, is an iconic example of midcentury modern design. The best-known design is the Lotus collection, which can be found in tons of bright colors. There are whole websites dedicated to finding and collecting these pieces!

Fiestaware: Fiesta was introduced in 1936 by the Homer Laughlin China Works and was known for its vibrant colors, especially the pieces released during the 1960s. I suggest looking for bowls in different sizes, which can be used for everyday cooking, baking, and eating or displayed on shelves for some fun pops of color.

Heath Ceramics: Heath Ceramics started in California in 1948 by Edith and Brian Heath. The company is known for their iconic midcentury modern tableware and pottery, derived from California clay and designed for daily use. Today, Heath Ceramics continues to manufacture a variety of products, from classic tableware and ceramics to handcrafted tile.

Krenit: Designed Herbert Krenchel for Danish design firm Normann Copenhagen, Krenit enamel bowls are highly coveted by vintage collectors. They are great examples of understated mid-mod design, with a simple, solid black exterior and colorful enamel interior.

Pyrex: During the 1950s and 1960s many new colors and patterns were introduced to the Pyrex line, and I suggest doing some online research to find your favorites. (Some are shown on the left.) You can collect matching sets or create your own unique collection. I love that Pyrex dishes often come with corresponding glass lids, which makes them ideal for storing leftover food and reducing the use of plastics.

W hether your dining area is its own separate room or just a space you carve out when it's time to eat, you can make it feel midcentury modern. With materials, shapes, lighting, and color choices, there are simple guideposts that will signal mid-mod to anyone who gathers around your table—or wherever it is you choose to dine.

Dine With Style

First things first: You'll need somewhere to sit, and somewhere to put your food. While classic MCM table and chair guideposts are discussed in chapter 1 (pages 40–41), I thought it would be helpful to discuss them specifically in regard to the dining area.

CELEBRATE CLEAN LINES AND CURVES

For both dining tables and chairs, minimalism reigns supreme for a midcentury modern feel. You can take your cues from the design greats, such as Eero Saarinen, and opt for styles that feature a singular tulip-shaped base instead of four legs. Not only do pedestals reduce the reduce visual noise of table and chair legs, giving the impression that the furniture is floating, but they also help create more space for limbs when it's limited. The minimal aesthetic can also apply to the arms of chairs—many MCM styles do without them, in favor of more simple, curved designs.

LOOK TO TRADITIONAL BASE MATERIALS

Many of the clean lines and curves present in classic midcentury modern furniture were possible because of the materials they were made from, including bentwood, which was first used in the 1950s and 1960s as a new way to build furniture. There is a lack of decorative details, and instead the wood is formed, almost like a sculpture, into the furniture shape desired. When applied to dining chairs, like those seen in a client's space on page 129, the result feels organic. Something as boring as a chair you sit in to eat your cereal becomes a work of art and its own visual moment. Plastic and fiberglass were used to create dining furniture in the same way. While bentwood spoke to the organic, nature-inspired design, these manmade materials felt futuristic. Plastic and fiberglass are great choices for busy families—they're durable (and wipe-able) and perfect for those with children and pets. When it comes to tabletops, marble, wood (teak or walnut), and colored laminate are all great options.

There are many manufacturers of dining room furniture that created a plethora of designs in the midcentury period, which were made to last and, because of their amazing craftsmanship, can still look new today. They were typically constructed of all wood, from teak to walnut to oak, rather than the plywood or pressed wood of many contemporary pieces. When out and about and online, look for the following manufacturers and designers:

Broyhill, specifically their Brasilia collection
Carl Hansen & Søn
Fritz Hansen
Heywood-Wakefield
Lane Furniture
J. L. Møller

This classic midcentury tulip dining set was sourced secondhand. The bright upholstery was still in great shape, and the color pops against the deep blue of the fireplace. The sputnik chandelier helps separate the dining area from the kitchen in this open-concept space.

MIX AND MATCH SEATING STYLES

I am not really a matchy-matchy type of person. I like to mix things up. I think a combination of materials, textures, colors, and shapes can make a room more interesting—and it can be a more affordable way to instill mid-mod charm in your dining room than buying a set of four to six matching chairs. In my home, I tend to bring in different pieces of furniture as they come into my life, whether it's from taking advantage of a warehouse sale and scooping up some discounted pieces or stumbling upon an old set of chairs at a local garage sale (or maybe even ones sitting on the side of the road!).

Layering multiple types and styles of furniture into a room is a great way to add history and interest to your space. I've mixed different designs, from molded plastic chairs to leather-and-wood chairs to upholstered chairs, all around the same dining table. You can use an anchoring furniture piece, such as a round or oval dining table, to set the midcentury modern style, and then bring in two pairs of different chairs, or the same set of chairs but in different colors. Find a unifying factor, whether it's a color scheme, a type of wood (like walnut, oak, or teak), or a material like plastic to pair with something complementary.

EMBRACE UPHOLSTERY AND CUSHIONS

Another classic way to channel midcentury modern design in your dining chairs is to choose ones that are upholstered, like those we used in a dining room in Los Altos, California. The seat of the chair provides the visual interest, while the rest of the room is left relatively simple and unadorned. I'll talk about the use of color more in this chapter (page 145), but your chair cushions are a fantastic way to bring in some fun or help make the furniture more cohesive to the surroundings, especially in a mixed-used area.

In this busy household with kids, it was important to have durable, easy-to-clean furniture. Instead of dining chairs that were all the same color, we opted for plastic shell chairs in a mix of black and white. The black chairs match the black palette of the kitchen space and the gorgeous, modern pendant light, so the color helps to unify the two adjacent spaces.

Make a Statement with Lighting

Even if you don't have the square footage for a separate dining room, hanging a sculptural light fixture over the table is a great way to bring midcentury modern feel into the space or delineate a separate area—plus, it's always important to have good lighting when you're eating. We've gone over the classic pendant styles to choose from: futuristic atomic or Sputnik, other more geometric shades, sculptural bubble lamps, or simple globe or bowl-like shapes. Even if nothing else in your space is mid-mod, a showstopping statement light will infuse the whole room with the feel of the era. Aim to have thirty to thirty-six inches between the tabletop and the bottom of the light fixture. This height allows for those gathered around the table to see one another comfortably when seated.

If you don't have the setup for a pendant light, you can still make an MCM impact with wall sconces, a floor lamp in a corner, or even two table lamps on top of a sideboard or buffet.

Laminate is a great family-friendly material to use in your dining area. It's water resistant and durable, so daily spills and messes are no problem. Many laminate dining tables come with a pedestal-style base or wood legs, like the one shown here.

Many plastic or fiberglass side chairs can double as indoor dining chairs, so you can get two types of seating for the price of one. Additionally, they are usually designed to be stacked when not in use, which is great for small homes where space is limited.

Use Accents to Set the Mood

There are a few ways to bring midcentury modern color and influences into the dining room, many of which won't break the bank.

Add pops of color: In addition to adding color with your seat cushions, you can set your table with plates, bowls, and napkins in midcentury hues. You can also decorate with midcentury-inspired artwork, paint an accent wall, put up some wallpaper, or hang a tapestry to bring the room together.

Create a tablescape: I love creating a tablescape to bring life to a dining room—and the best part is, they're so easy to change to reflect your moods or needs. Tablescapes are a great way to signal your intent if your dining room is a multifunctional space. Start with a fun table runner and then add in mid-mod touches. I like using white ceramic vases to create a base layer, then adding in colorful ceramics. Vintage glassware, such as Blenko glassware, can help you bring in true midcentury modern design, even in spaces that are not full of MCM furniture.

Store and display: An MCM credenza is as useful as it is beautiful. Use it to store extra dishware, glassware, tablescape materials, and whatever else needs hiding. Display fun tchotchkes, plants, and artwork on top to bring personality and life into the room. If you don't have space for a credenza, you can hang shelves, like we did for a client in Phoenix (page 130), which provides a surface to decorate without taking up a large footprint.

If you have limited space for a dining table, look for styles that are adjustable. There are many midcentury modern inspired tables that fold out or come with extensions that can be used when guests visit. Fold-up tables are great, too, and some can be attached to a wall and expanded only when needed, barely taking up any space when not in use. Even a classic MCM coffee table, like those discussed on page 41, can become a casual dining area when space is at a premium. Scatter some pillows with mid-mod designs on the floor for multifunctional seating.

Do you have a shelf that needs a refresh? Perhaps an area of a dresser or credenza? No matter how small, you can make any surface a showstopper.

Gather some decorative things from around the house (for some reason, I like to use odd numbers). These can range from a book to a small vase to a favorite framed photo to a tree branch from your yard. Plants and planters can add a touch of green and a bit of nature, too.

Just like designing and styling a larger room, it's all about creating a few different layers and levels, even if you are arranging a handful of items on a shelf or small table. I like to start with a book, whether it's a current read or a vintage book or coffee table book, then stack a plant and planter on top. A candle or small vase next to them rounds out the collection and then all of sudden you have taken a blank space and created a visual collection that shows your personality.

If entertaining at home is your specialty, creating a home bar setup is a fun way to bring midcentury-inspired design into a space, no matter how small. A bar cart in a mid-mod design is a great option because they're mobile, so you can store them out of the way when not in use. A small table, cabinet, or a floating shelf can also be used to store and display bottles and glassware. For various clients, we have even created bar areas that utilize existing kitchen cabinets with added mirrored glass to make the space seem bigger—and for a bit of sparkle. If you can't install anything permanently, a mirror hung over or leaned atop your setup can provide the same vibe.

You can give nods to the era by displaying vintage glass-ware, even if the furniture itself is a different style. Look for funky barware from local antique shops. Vintage bar-ware was often designed with metal accents and patterns and is a low-budget way to bring some glitz into your cocktail presentations. Don't forget useful items like an ice bucket or pitcher, which are also easy to find in mid-mod designs.

ABOVE: In my home, a family heirloom liquor cabinet (not midcentury modern, but special to our family) provides additional bar storage and a spot for my MCM collectibles.

OPPOSITE: A vintage bar sink and MCM dresser were combined to create this unique home cocktail bar area. The glass shelves are almost invisible, and the bold wallpaper that matches the sink is a fun touch.

6 | CREATING A MIDCENTURY MODERN
BATHROOM

hat are some classic signifiers of original midcentury bathrooms? Color! Many MCM bathrooms were traditionally pink, blue, or green. From the tile to the toilet to the sink and tub. Many also featured clever storage, such as built-in toothbrush holders, a razorblade depository, an integrated tissue box holder, and the timeless recessed mirrored medicine cabinet. So what can you do to make your bathroom feel midcentury? We encourage clients to keep original features of a space (renovations are expensive!) and focus on a few design elements that have a big impact.

Adding fun touches to this bathroom allowed us to give the space a modern feel without a big renovation. These clients are passionate about aviation, so vintage artwork was a great way to bring in midcentury modern sensibility to the space.

An Inspired Sink Area

VANITIES

Midcentury bathroom vanities were often very simple and were made from painted or stained walnut or oak, with slab doors and a laminate countertop—oftentimes with small flecks in the laminate to give some subtle sparkle. They had simple drawers or sliding doors with shelving inside. Sometimes they had small conical legs; other times they were mounted onto the wall for a floating, uncluttered effect. To get the same feel, look for vanities that are simple, without chunky legs or decorative details.

If you are restoring or keeping an existing vanity, paint can do wonders. In a ranch-style home in Hollister, California, the existing cabinets were Shaker style, with trim work. To save money, we kept the doors and gave them a fresh coat of white paint. Adding a bright white quartz top—a more modern nod to laminate countertops—and a simple rounded rectangular sink helped emulate an old-school midcentury vibe.

For another bathroom, a pale pink vanity was one of the first selections for the new design, serving as the anchor point for the rest of the bathroom materials. Distinctly retro details like recessed door and drawer handles and hairpin legs make this piece the fabulous star of the room. With vibrant pink in the space, we paired neutrals in creams, white, and warm grays to balance out the room's palette.

Bathrooms can often be tight on space and storage, especially when whole families are sharing one. To help avoid clutter, look for vanities with deep drawer storage or additional shelving below the main compartments. Open shelving is a great place for storage bins dedicated to each person or for surplus basics like toilet paper and cleaning supplies. Look for bins in fun colors to complement the space or provide a pop of vibrancy.

TOP: In a home in Castro Valley, California, we re-created the original wood slab-style vanity in white oak. To give it a truly authentic feel, we sourced vintage V-shaped hardware online. The cabinet pulls had been removed from an old furniture piece, which gave us the perfect way to make something new feel old.

BOTTOM: The use of wood slats was prevalent in midcentury design, so as a nod to that feature, we used them on the bathroom vanity in this home in Daly City, California. They add visual interest without taking all the attention from the other elements of the room.

MIRRORS AND MEDICINE CABINETS

Much like with the vanity itself, stay away from fussy details and keep medicine cabinets and mirrors simple—whether rectangular, oval, round, or square. Today there are a lot of great retro mirror reproductions that look like they were plucked right out of 1950s or 1960s bathrooms. They have clean lines and are an easy, relatively affordable way to give a midcentury look to space.

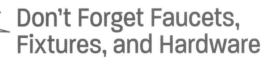

Don't Forget Faucets, Fixtures, and Hardware

There's no need to reinvent the wheel when it comes to bathroom fixtures. Polished chrome works for everything from medicine cabinets to faucets to shower and tub fixtures. It's also a good choice for towel rods and toilet-paper holders. Avoid overly ornate styles and steer toward designs with simple round, circular, or square bases.

However, you can also use your hardware to make a statement. In my bathroom design, since I brought in small mosaic tile in a neutral white, I knew I wanted to contrast the white with a midcentury modern hue. I decided to install a classic mid-mod single-hole faucet with a simple lever. Instead of a polished chrome finish, I selected a vibrant orange, combining a simple faucet with a pop of bold midcentury color to make it more interesting.

Level Up Your Lighting

It was common to find midcentury modern lighting in polished chrome, black, and brass. There are a number of contemporary manufacturers that create authentic midcentury modern styles in a combination of finishes and colors, which allows you to customize them to fit your home and palette. Have some fun with shapes like space-inspired chandeliers, bowties, cones, and globes.

Contemporary manufacturers like Cedar & Moss, Lucent Lightshop, Dutton Brown, Roll & Hill (all made in the USA), Tom Dixon, Muuto, and David Trubridge, incorporate mid-mod characteristics. For more inspiration, check out the work of these iconic MCM lighting designers and manufacturers.

Alvar Aalto
Artek
Artemide
Achille Castiglioni
FLOS Lighting
Poul Henningsen
Arne Jacobsen
Kartell
George Kovacs
Greta Magnusson-
  Grossman
Serge Mouille
George Nelson
Verner Panton
Louis Poulsen

Transform the Space with Tile

There are several companies that manufacture their tile in the United States, and purchasing from them supports domestic labor and craftsmanship. Some of these tile companies have been in around since the midcentury and use the same artisanal process. Several manufacturers on this list produce their products from post-consumer recycled materials and domestically sourced materials, making them an eco-friendly and sustainable choice.

Clayhaus
Fireclay Tile
Heath Ceramics
Heritage Tile
LIVDEN
MADE by Ann Sacks
Mercury Mosaics
Modwalls
Pratt and Larson

Historically, the same tile was installed throughout a bathroom, from the floor to walls. You have to be willing to commit, but taking this approach is a surefire way to bring back your space back to the midcentury.

Square or small mosaic tiles in the same color family, set in straight lines, like what we did for a client's fantastic pink bathroom in Phoenix, Arizona (at right), is a good choice for allover tiling because it doesn't overwhelm like a larger size or more complicated pattern would. What's great about a tile selection like this is that it is readily available at big-box suppliers, making it an affordable way to cover a large amount of space for a uniquely midcentury vibe.

If allover tile isn't your style or in your budget, pick an accent wall or smaller space to splurge on and use a simple, affordable subway tile in clean, straight lines for the remaining area. The eyes

STAND HERE
AND THINK ABOUT
SOMEONE
YOU LOVE

will be drawn to the bold focal point, so you'll want a more neutral or subtle tone everywhere else for balance. In my bathroom (page 164), I sourced specialty tile at a fraction of the cost by purchasing overstock seconds tile from a local tile maker. When approaching a project where you plan to put together different tiles, try to stick with a common denominator—in my case, all the tile on the feature wall is the same shape and size (hexagons) but is in different colors. I then opted for white mosaic tile for the rest of the space.

For those who want their space to be tranquil and spa-like, forgo the bright colors and instead look for tile with interesting texture in peaceful pastel palettes. In Castro Valley, California (at right), a client's bathroom was mid-mod originally, including pastel wallpaper in the bathtub area. When planning the new design, we wanted to honor the home's unique roots. Instead of wallpaper (which doesn't work too well near a bathtub!) we chose a patterned, dimensional tile in a soothing, mint tone. The tile was paired with long, narrow gray tile to balance the pale green.

If you're not looking to redo your walls, focus on the floors. Larger terrazzo-look tiles can help give a nice baseline for the other design elements, such as specialty tilework or unique light fixtures. In our Warren, Vermont project (page 169, bottom), to save on the renovation budget, we redid only half of the bathroom, leaving the tub area alone, and let the floors provide the visual accent: a linear pattern layered on top of a pink hexagon shape, a playful way to bring in color and fun.

OPPOSITE: Condo and apartment bathrooms can feel small, but with the right materials, you can make the room feel larger than it is. For a petite condo bathroom, we drew from midcentury shapes by selecting a triangular tile. With a contrasting bright-white grout, the installation creates a fun, modern pattern, which provides a defining visual moment while still feeling serene.

BOTTOM: These clients have a passion for all things midcentury modern and frequently visit places like Palm Springs, so we tiled the shower floor in graphic black-and-white terrazzo—a distinctly midcentury modern material. To save on budget, we went with a simple white subway tile for the shower walls, installed vertically to make the room seem taller.

To give a nod to this home's original pink tile, we brought in a touch of pink through a multicolored triangular pattern. The old storage nook above the toilet was kept after the renovation but painted matte black, which serves to give a visual break from the busyness of the wall, as well as serve as the perfect spot to bring in plants and extra towel storage.

I'M TOTALLY INTIMIDATED BY TILE. WHAT ARE SOME THINGS I SHOULD KNOW?

Tile is a classic midcentury modern material (turn to page 36 for more discussion), and it's a surefire way to give a space a certain look. When planning a midcentury modern–inspired bathroom, the tile is what guides us, whether it's bringing back a retro feel with pink tile, grounding a space with understated floor tiles, or adding texture with dimensional tile. Keep in mind that rectangular tiles can be installed lengthwise or vertically. Install tile horizontally to make the walls feel wider; install tile vertically to make the space seem taller and draw the eye upward.

Here's a look at the different kinds of tile you might come across:

Ceramic and porcelain tile: Both ceramic and porcelain tiles are made from clay. Handcrafted ceramic tile is still produced by hand by several domestic US manufacturers (see page 164). Porcelain tile is made from a more refined clay and fired at higher temperatures, so it becomes denser and water permeable. Handcrafted tile is created from recycled raw materials such as clay and granite. The tile produced today has roots in midcentury modern ceramics and craft, helping bring historic authenticity back into homes.

Dimensional or 3D tile: Dimensional tile is formed through molds and, instead of flat surfaces, has a three-dimensional quality. Installing several dimensional pieces of tile really brings multifaceted depth to the pattern.

Hand-painted and patterned tile: Hand-painted tile can give a flat surface an added depth, with pattern play and design painted directly onto the tile surface. Cement and porcelain tiles also come in patterned options: The designs are imprinted onto the surface at a more budget-friendly price than hand-painted versions.

Glass tile: Contemporary glass tile is sometimes created from recycled glass and can be found in both matte and glossy finishes.

TOP: This tile actually has the pattern printed onto it. We opted to install it in a more randomized design to give the feel of a custom mural to the shower wall.

MIDDLE: In a small guest bathroom, we installed large-format black slate-like porcelain tile with accents of inlaid brass. Using a larger format means fewer grout lines and an almost seamless look. A larger tile also makes the floor space seem larger than it really is. Elegant brass inlay was popular in midcentury modern flooring, and since it's expensive, using it in a room with a small footprint is a cost-effective way to incorporate it.

If tile isn't in the budget, opt for paint or wallpaper for a quick midcentury modern makeover. Integrate pastels or bright oranges and turquoises with paint or vintage-inspired wallpaper patterns. For bathrooms, keep in mind there will be water and moisture and look for moisture-resistant wallpapers designed specifically for humid spaces. If you're painting, try color blocking or repeat a simple shape or pattern on a wall to create your own faux wallpaper. Painter's tape plus a gallon of paint is all you need to create your own unique designs.

In a guest bathroom in San Jose, CA, the black and white tile features a repeating hexagonal shape, inspired by classic Palm Springs midcentury modern design found everywhere from iconic houses to retro boutique hotels. A busy pattern like this works well for a petite space. We love putting bold designs in small spaces, especially powder rooms, because it provides a surprising "wow" moment for guests.

Whatever our souls are made of,
his and mine are the same.

EMILY BRONTË

Shower curtains are a fantastic low-budget way to add a midcentury modern touch. Look for curtains with color blocking in MCM hues like aqua and orange. There are some great online companies that allow you to create your own pattern and print it on whatever you'd like. Repeat a simple shape like a triangle, square, or half-moon in monochromatic tones or play with contrasting colors. Another fun DIY project is to color block on fabric yourself. Find a simple shape on a rubber stamp, select a few fabric inks, and stamp away!

Add Pizzaz with Practical Items

Even on the smallest budget, you can bring some midcentury style to your bathroom—and let your personality shine, too. Retro-inspired patterns, earthy ceramics, pops of color, and sleek, modern lines are great finishing touches. To bring warmth into the space, look for items that are made from wood or are in earthy or dark tones. Shelves, stools, and cabinets made from teak or bamboo can warm up a space and balance any bold colors you incorporate.

When it comes to bathroom accessories, don't forget to think of both fashion and function. I love bringing color and pattern in through hand towels, bathmats, and shower curtains. They are necessary for the room, so why not make them fun? Toothbrush holders, soap dispensers, storage baskets, and towel hooks are practical but can also be an opportunity to add some pizzazz. A decorative tray can be layered with a candle or a vase of flowers. You can even repurpose items from other rooms in your house to make the space feel complete. I took a small ceramic plate from a big-box retailer that was in my kitchen and now use it as a place to put my rings when I wash my hands.

OPPOSITE: A vintage hand towel holder, with a distinct starburst design brings authentic midcentury fun to a gray hand towel.

When space is limited, going vertical is a great way to keep things off the floor. Shelves, wall hooks, and even a storage ladder can help keep your bathroom tidy. Utilizing the space within your walls is another way to maximize every inch of storage. If you can install a recessed medicine cabinet or storage nook you'll be rewarded with a midcentury built-in look that's super functional for busy families.

Another family-friendly addition to your bathroom that can give a mid-mod vibe might be unexpected. Towel bars in polished chrome, sometimes stacked one above another to allow for hanging multiple towels at once, were popular in traditional midcentury bathrooms. It's an easy design feature you can include in your bathroom, with the added bonus of multiuser functionality. You can make this feature more modern and cozier by choosing heated towel warmers and towel racks. Not only do they serve as storage, but they are designed to quickly dry damp towels, which is more hygienic (water = bacteria!). This is a great way to get towels dried and off the floor, a huge help when you are sharing your bathroom with children.

7

CREATING A MIDCENTURY MODERN
ENTRYWAY AND
OUTDOOR SPACE

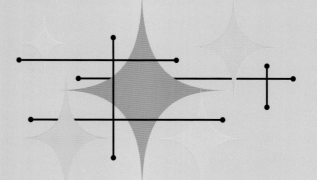

We've covered
the different
ways you can
bring some midcentury modern
style to the interior rooms in
your home, but let's not forget
the entryways, exteriors, and
outdoor areas. After all, they are
the first things people see when
they visit and can help express
a welcoming, mid-mod tone
before they even get inside.

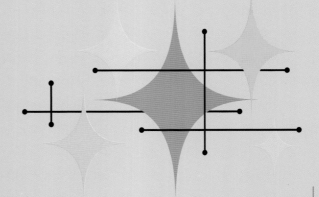

Designate a Drop Zone

Since your entryway sets the initial impression for the rest of your home, I always aim to keep it stylish and uncluttered. That's why it's key to create a "drop zone" for those everyday items like shoes, keys, coats, and bags that can wreak havoc if left unchecked.

There are so many fun midcentury modern–inspired accessories just for this purpose, including multifunctional storage and bench systems, which provide a place to remove your shoes as well as store them. Even if your home doesn't have a big foyer, all it takes is a designated area with organization accessories: Minimalist coat racks or wall hooks are ideal for wrangling jackets and bags, and a tabletop surface, such as a sleek console, works as a place to throw your keys or sunglasses. The iconic Eames Hang-It-All, like the one used in clients' Arizona entry (at left), was specifically designed for children and uses colorful balls instead of hooks to be gentler on clothing. Other midcentury-style choices include a "fin system" of wood pegs. On their own, the wood pegs look like sculpture, but when needed they provide multi-jacket or -bag storage while also looking sleek.

You'll also want to add to some personality to this area with artwork, plants, and lighting. If you're tight on space, strategically using wallpaper, paint, rugs, and other decor to define the area is a great way to carve out an entryway even if it doesn't technically exist. These are all fun ways to add a touch of MCM spirit.

Even if you don't have a separate entryway or mudroom, you can create one with just a few items. When my kids were young, I was always amazed at how organized their classrooms were: thirty little coats and backpacks hanging on hooks in neat rows. Coat hooks are perfect for organizing not only outerwear but also things like dog leashes, umbrellas, and bags. They have a minimal footprint, so they're perfect for small spaces. For households with younger children, hang a set of hooks at a lower height so the kids can hang up their own coats. If they can do this at school, why not at home, too?

In my home, shoes come off first thing upon entering, but we don't have a closet nearby. Instead we opted for a modern, minimalist metal storage stand, which can house a handful of family members' shoes. The rest are stored away, but the daily-use pairs can be easily accessed. We sit at the bright orange mid-mod bench to take off or put on shoes, but it also doubles as a staging spot for a work bag or backpack. Instead of a small doormat, I placed a long runner underneath both items to provide more coverage and define our drop zone. The runner is machine washable, which is necessary when dealing with dirty sneakers all the time.

Channel Mid-Mod Curb Appeal

There are many ways to bring midcentury modern style to your home's exterior, some requiring a bigger budget, like building or painting walls, while others can be as simple as adding a vibrant doormat and coordinating planter outside your front door.

Original midcentury modern homes were typically built from a mix of materials like concrete and brick, and they featured exterior wood framing and board and batten or pinstripe-style paneling. In homes with wood siding, the wood was sometimes painted in nature-inspired hues such as sage green, taupe, or brown, and combined with architectural accents such as Roman brick, decorative concrete breeze-blocks, or stonework. Our clients' original midcentury modern home in Alameda, California, is situated along a lagoon waterway. The entrance to the property

For clients in Alameda, California, we kept to the home's original white color scheme from the 1960s, which is fitting for a home situated on water and exudes a marina-vacation feel. We then added a bright pop of color with the door.

is marked by an iconic curved breeze-block wall, which provides privacy to their courtyard and gives a defining structure to their home. Original architectural features like this are hard to find in contemporary construction, making the design and build of the home all the more special.

Today, you can pull from those nature-inspired color palettes and then bring in a bold accent color with your door, such as pumpkin, lemon, or turquoise. For a more dramatic exterior color palette, grays and charcoals can be very striking house colors. A client's house in San Jose, California, was originally clad in wide wood siding. When redesigning, we wanted to blend a bit of California modern style with traditional midcentury modern materials to give a nod to the past while presenting a more modern feel. The result is a charcoal-painted wood-paneled exterior with gorgeous cedar siding in the entryway shown on page 186.

To create a pool enclosure, new breeze-blocks were stacked (with a plexiglass partition) and paired with a powder-coated orange metal door. The metal sofa and table mimic the lines in the door to help make the space feel intentional.

EXPERIMENT WITH EXTERIOR DECOR

If a big exterior paint job or landscaping project isn't in the plans right now, try smaller, budget makeovers, like a graphic door mat. For our home, we used to have a standing mailbox that was very ornate (pagoda-like) and a bit distracting. We replaced it with a mail slot, which is more traditional for the time period. For clients in Los Altos, California, we installed a mailbox with a boxy, modern shape and a pop of color. If this is a change you can make, look for clean lines and fun colors like pink, turquoise, orange, or red, and make your mailperson's day a bit brighter.

Painting your front door can have the same effect. And don't worry too much about the color. Paint is easy to redo, especially on a door, so pick a hue that makes you happy and go for it! A bright yellow door pops against the charcoal-gray exterior of a home in Walnut Creek, California, but we've also had clients paint only the interior of their front door, while keeping the exterior a more muted shade.

For a midcentury home in Warren, Vermont (page 176), we really wanted the exterior to blend peacefully with the incredible landscape surrounding the property, keeping with the midcentury idea of letting nature influence aesthetics and function. This is why we chose to stain the exterior wood paneling in muted charcoal and gray-brown tones. The home's original stacked-stone fireplace is an outstanding focal point and when combined with the neutral exterior, the home's classic mid-mod roofline stands out among the nearby trees. A sidelight brings in natural light and is an architectural feature found in many original midcentury modern homes.

Other ways to give touches of mid-mod design include switching up your house numbers and choosing era-appropriate lighting. For house numbers, look for numbers in a sans serif font, which gives off a clean look and is drawn from original midcentury graphic design and architecture. For lighting, look for globe lights and sconces instead of your typical porch light.

For our clients in San Jose, California (at left), we used all three: a bright orange door, sans serif numbers set against warm wood siding, and a statement-making globe pendant light, which matches a twin interior globe entryway light. The result is undeniably midcentury modern.

DETERMINE THE SPACE'S FUNCTION

Similar to interior rooms, it's important to determine what your goals are with an outdoor space, because even with just a balcony or fire escape, you can create your own outdoor entertaining area with a midcentury feel. Do you want a place to dine? A place to sit and lounge? A place for kids to play or for a furry family member to run free? Decide how you want to use your space, and then carve out and define those areas. You can use things like plants and planters, rock walls, furniture, outdoor rugs, or even lighting to help delineate the different zones.

For seating, your furniture can be as luxurious as an MCM-inspired outdoor sofa and matching dining set or as simple as sleek, weather-friendly folding chairs and a small metal table. For more robust furniture, keep things simple. For an outdoor space in San Jose, California (page 191), a simple, neutral-colored outdoor lounge set with metal a framework lends comfortable seating to the area. And the bold, graphic black and white rug brings visual interest and helps define the area as a dedicated lounge space.

Whereas for a home in Hollister, California, shown here, the outdoor space was designed with maximum relaxation and entertaining in mind. The most accessible area is located right off the home's main sliding door, so we placed a dining set in a central spot. To make the most of the mild California climate, an outdoor bar and kitchen space is adjacent to the dining area. The flow of the spaces makes it easy to bring food and drinks from either setup. On the opposite end of the yard, there is a stock tank pool and deck (page 190)—ideal for a cool dip during warm summer days or nights—far enough from the dining and cooking areas for them to retain their separate functions.

The homeowners of this California ranch home love visiting Palm Springs, which is the primary design inspiration for their home's interior design as well as the backyard design and custom stock tank pool.

Perhaps dining outside isn't the goal for your space. One or two chairs to sit and relax in might be all you need. To channel the mid-mod minimalist, floating principle, install a hanging chair or hammock. If you need more of a flex space, put down an outdoor rug or some artificial turf that can be moved when not in use. You can bring out a few floor pillows or cushions to lounge when needed, then bring them back inside. Choosing small, flexible pieces is helpful in this situation: a stool that doubles as a side table or a patio set that can be folded and packed away when space is limited.

Since many outdoor items are made from metal or plastic, look for fun, bright mid-mod colors or paint your own! For comfort, you might want to add pillows or cushions, which give another opportunity to add some MCM charm with patterned fabrics or contrasting colors. Ceramic or cement stools also emulate midcentury modern designs and are multifunctional.

Create an outdoor screen or partition. Part of the architecture of my courtyard-style midcentury modern house features a framed partial glass wall that provides privacy from the outside but still gives a bit of transparency to my front exterior (page 193). You can create your own decorative outdoor screen with wood pieces to create see-through slats. If you aren't feeling DIY, several companies make portable metal screens, which are nice for areas such as private balconies. These portable privacy panels let some light through the shapes while still creating a visual barrier. A bunch of tall grassy plants, planted in tall planters is another way to add privacy and nature to a balcony area.

For another take on outdoor furniture, look for woven items. Woven outdoor furniture was very prevalent in the 1950s to 1970s. These outdoor collections were typically made from materials such as plastic cord or natural rattan and are often found in vintage photos of beach vacations or poolside parties. The Acapulco chair is a classic design made with a steel base and woven plastic cords wound around the frame to create a chair that is quite comfortable—and colorful. In my yard, shown on the opposite page, I mixed a vintage Acapulco chair base that my husband restrung with a midcentury-inspired rattan outdoor sofa.

For fashion and function, don't forget about your lighting. From portable globe lanterns to string lights, you can infuse MCM into your outdoor ambience. Some companies even make battery-operated or rechargeable outdoor floor and table lamps, which, if in a mid-mod shape, can signal to the era without any worry about cords or electrical outlets.

The basic form of many midcentury modern furniture pieces was a simple wood box or woven frame with a cushion over it, which makes it super easy for you to create your own inspired outdoor furniture using this principle.

WHAT ARE SOME KEY MCM OUTDOOR FURNITURE PIECES, STYLES, AND MATERIALS I SHOULD LOOK FOR?

If you are just getting started with midcentury modern furniture, here are some styles that work well to establish MCM design in your outdoor spaces.

Rope-and-metal chairs (Acapulco chairs)

Metal circular/slice chairs (in the style of Salterini)

Acrylic or fiberglass furniture

Wood or metal frames with cushions

Sculptural metal (Bertoia chairs)

Concrete tables, stools, firepits, and side tables

Molded or formed plastic

Powder-coated metal

Woven or rattan pieces

Malm outdoor fireplaces

If you have little ones at home, how about a midcentury modern outdoor playhouse for the kids? Midcentury modern houses were all about simplicity and clean lines, so even a small, simple house or tree house, constructed from plywood, can become a mini-modernist's outdoor play space to dream up their own adventures.

INCORPORATE PLANTS AND GREENERY

Midcentury-inspired landscaping takes its cues from the overall minimalist design aesthetic of the time and often features concrete pads, rock pathways, and a mix of structured plantings. The placement of the greenery almost feels mathematical, like in the preciseness of the succulents in our San Jose clients' front yard. Famous midcentury properties, such as Fallingwater designed by architect Frank Lloyd Wright, were sometimes concepted around a nearby rocks, trees, or in this case, a waterfall, which allowed nature to rule both indoors and outside: The home was built around the site's natural elements, not the other way around.

For smaller-scale greenery, look for textured ceramic planters to bring in a sculptural influence, such as the ceramic designs by artists Kat Hutter and Roger Lee (page 200). Their work features playful colors and pattern mixing, combined with the organic nature commonly found in midcentury modern sculpture and ceramics. Or you can go for monochromatic brightly colored planters with simple curves. Most plant stands are inherently MCM inspired and fuss-free, with thin or hairpin legs and clean lines. If space is limited, look for hanging planters or ones that you can mount to an outside wall. Even on a small balcony area, you can create a mini greenhouse. Using planters for your greenery is helpful here and if one plant doesn't work out, you can always try to swap it out for another!

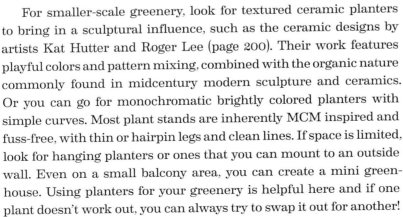

Take old or plain planters and give them a mid-mod make-over. I spray-painted a basic oversized big-box retailer planter in a bright blue. Then I planted a pink cordyline plant, which gives a contrasting color and a bold shape to grow out of the planter.

Planters don't have to be made from ceramic or plastic. Woven baskets and metal containers also work well. Just make sure there are drainage holes for watering and something underneath to catch any watering overflow. This is a fun, easy way to give thrift-store items new life!

Embrace Outdoor Entertaining

When it comes time to entertain, think back to the kitchen and dining room chapters (pages 124 and 145) for inspiration. Colorful trays are great for transporting food and beverages outside. Look for lacquered or plastic trays. There are a lot of fun designs for outdoor tableware and glassware that are nonbreakable and come in fun midcentury modern colors. And you can bring in even more color with cloth napkins, which are an excellent eco-friendly addition to entertaining.

I created an outdoor coffee table by mounting leftover cement tiles to an old metal coffee-table frame. Reuse shops are great places to search for leftover building materials like tile, which can be applied to other furniture pieces to create your own unique design. When reusing metal frames or furniture, look for metal-specific paints, which are designed to be rust resistant, key to any metal furniture that has to weather the outdoor elements.

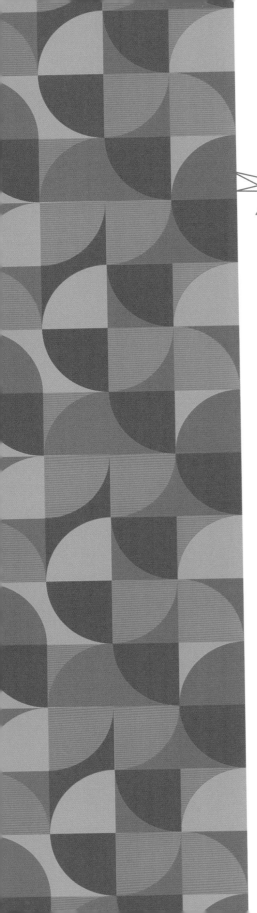

RESOURCES

Shopping Sustainably

In today's world full of mass-produced furniture and decor, I believe that choosing sustainable options whenever possible is more important than ever. Fortunately, much like when it comes to adding mid-mod touches to your home, it only takes a few approachable guideposts and ideas to help reduce your carbon footprint.

WHY SHOP SECONDHAND?

What better way to bring a vintage vibe into your home than by giving old treasures a new life? I am an avid estate sale enthusiast, vintage store shopper, and thrifter. My obsession for old and recycled items started back in middle and high school, when friends and I would traverse across the Bay to "go thrifting." We would take BART out to San Francisco to visit vintage clothing shops in Haight-Ashbury or Berkeley. Then when I lived in Boston as a struggling ballerina, I would head to Cambridge for the "dollar-a-pound" clothing buys at a store named the Garment District. I loved the thrill of searching through the racks and piles of clothing for a unique piece to wear and love—plus the cost savings worked for my shoestring budget.

Nowadays, while I still can't resist a great secondhand outfit, I also always on the hunt vintage home goods. My collection ranges from a C. Jere brass sculpture by my fireplace to an Eames molded plywood screen. I may not have anything particular in mind when I pull over to the side of the road to see what's for sale at a local estate sale, but that mystery is the fun of the hunt!

What might seem old, worn, and worthless to someone else could end up the perfect addition to a home that's needs bit of mid-mod charm. Even if you don't find an exact piece by a famous designer, there are many similar designs created during the era by other makers. Which means you can get a great deal on a timeless piece that's made to last. Plus, you do good for the planet by keeping something out of a landfill and gain a unique piece to add to your home!

WHERE TO SHOP

From brick-and-mortar stores to online marketplaces to open-air markets, there are plenty of places to score amazing vintage or secondhand finds.

Antiques and flea markets: From smaller pop-ups to large-scale permanent operations, many markets often have regular schedules, such as monthly or semi-annually. Follow various markets on social media or subscribe to their newsletters to be reminded of upcoming events. For amazing midcentury modern finds, plan a trip to the Brimfield Antique Flea Markets in Massachusetts or visit the monthly Palm Springs Vintage Market in California.

Estate sales: Estate sales often advertise online or just with signage on neighborhood corners. Some websites aggregate a multitude of estate sales by location, all across the nation. You can search for events by different criteria, such as location and date, sign up for their newsletter so that you receive alerts anytime there is a new event nearby, and even shop from afar, through online auctions. You'll always want to arrive to estate sales as early as possible so you can take full advantage of the offerings. Note, too, that you'll have to pay up front and transport the items yourself.

Garage sales: Garage sales are fantastic places to shop for vintage items, usually for lower prices than other options. If the pieces are in rough shape, they make great starter projects to try out DIY skills, since the monetary investment isn't too high.

Online marketplaces: Thanks to websites like Facebook Marketplace, Craigslist, and eBay, you can now source pretty much anything you're looking for from other people who want to sell it. These sites are pretty easy to use, but always make sure to use common sense when it comes to picking items up, and do your research to avoid being taken advantage of. There are also myriad digital marketplaces specifically for MCM or vintage items, so spend some time clicking around until you come across your perfect find.

Thrift stores: Try your local secondhand or consignment store. From clothing to housewares, you can almost always find something amazing and affordable, though you might have to spend some time scouring the racks and shelves to find what you're looking for.

WHAT TO LOOK FOR

If you are new to the world of thrifting and vintage shopping, the sheer number of possibilities can be overwhelming, so here are some tips for finding midcentury treasures.

Know the right keywords. When looking for vintage items online, I start with broader search terms such as *midcentury modern furniture*, or *midcentury modern lighting* to get to a category of products. From there, I can zone in on the particular piece I'm looking for, such as *lounge chairs, dining tables, credenzas, sideboards,* or *bedroom furniture*. Then I focus in on a particular style or design. Even if you don't plan on purchasing a piece by a famous designer or manufacturer, searching for iconic names like *Eames* or *Lane Furniture* or *Broyhill*, can bring up similar vintage pieces made in the spirit of such designers.

Do your research. Before heading out on the hunt, make sure you know what you're looking for and any telltale signs of authenticity. For example, some manufacturers used to stamp their company's name and logo on the bottom of pieces. Or you can save pictures on your phone of patterns and motifs you'd like to add to your collection. This is especially helpful for vintage tableware! Tracing pieces back to their original designers or manufacturers can be a helpful way to find more information on the specific piece, provide some baseline pricing, and help you make an informed decision on how much to spend on a vintage find. For online listings, check out any photos provided and if they don't have a of detail, ask for more. This way you can look out for any dings/nicks or damage and decide if they might affect how much you would like to pay for the piece.

Pay attention to materials. Look for midcentury and MCM-inspired furniture made from recycled plastics, solid wood (walnut or teak are popular), or fiberglass. These items are sturdy and made to last. In our kitchen, we have fiberglass counter stools that are seemingly indestructible. We don't have to worry about the kids scratching them or spilling anything on them.

Look beyond cosmetic issues. Just like old houses, see if a piece has "good bones." A scuffed wooden table or a rusted metal chair can often be brought back to life with some sanding (okay, a lot of sanding!) and finishing. You can cover a whole host of eyesores or completely change the appearance of something with some patience and paint!

Choose vintage versions when possible. Most authentic midcentury items are much better quality than their modern counterparts, which means you're making a better long-term investment.

Imperfect can be perfect. One of the first pieces of furniture we purchased when moved into our midcentury modern home was a scratched and water-stained wooden surfboard-shaped coffee table. It was maybe $70 at a garage sale. I always had a plan to refinish it but wanted to wait until our boys grew out of toddlerhood and elementary school before investing my time and energy in making it "perfect" again. But by keeping it in its less-than-ideal state, I never actually had to worry about anything happening to it, which gave a sense of freedom. Old, vintage, and imperfect furniture can be your friend!

Retailers, Artists, Designers, Manufacturers, and Inspiration

1stDibs
ABC Modern
Angela Adams
Ann Sacks
Antiques Colony
Atomic Ranch
Babyletto
Block Shop Textiles
Blu Dot
Burrow
Casara Modern
CB2
Cedar & Moss
Chairish
Chasing Paper
Chilewich
Circle & Line
Claire Åkebrand
Cle Tile
Design Within Reach
Docomomo US
ducduc
Dutton Brown
Eichler Network
Exactly Designs
Fab Habitat
Fermob
Fireclay Tile
FLOR
Floyd
Forge Hardware

Former Modern
Galanter & Jones
Geometry
Habita Wallpaper
HAY
Heath Ceramics
Heritage Tile
Hip Haven
Hygge & West
Industry West
Jacob Willard Home
Jen Hewett
Jessica Poundstone
Johanna Howard Home
Jon Morse
Jonathan Adler
Kat and Roger
LCDmodern
Lightology
Lisa Congdon
LIVDEN
Loll Designs
Lotta Jansdotter
Lucent Light Shop
Mercury Mosaics
Mid Mod Mich
Mid-Century Maurer
Midcentury LA
Midcentury Mobler
Mitzi
Mod Science

Modern Fabrics
Modern House Numbers
Modern Manor
Modernica
Modernism Week
Modwalls
Narrative Oak
Nordic Knots
Nugget
Orla Kiely
Phillip Jeffries
Practical Props
Radical Relics
Rejuvenation
Room & Board
Ruggable
Scandinavian Designs
Schoolhouse
Scout Living
Semihandmade
Skinny laMinx
Soda Pop Vintage
Spoonflower
Sunset Bazaar
Tilebar
Urban Americana
Vinteige View
West Elm
World Market
Zia Tile

ACKNOWLEDGMENTS

Creating this book is a dream come true, and I am grateful to an extensive network of kind and supportive people who made it happen. Thank you to all the wonderful people who started following our DIY blog in the early days and have continued over the years, many who have turned into dear friends and clients. Thank you, Dibble, for being my photographer-partner-in-crime for the past few years and agreeing to come along on this journey! Our synergy is second to none. Huge gratitude to the wonderful homeowners who entrusted me and my team to design their spaces and graciously allowed Chris and I to photograph and share their beautiful homes for this project. To my incredibly talented design team, Aisha, Olivia, and Garrett—your energy, passion for midcentury modern design, creativity, and enthusiasm are unparalleled. You make "going to work" not seem like work at all! Thank you to Aisha for working with me to create the gorgeous illustrations seen throughout the book. Props to Daniel and Declan for ensuring a number of these projects came to fruition and for never giving me a hard time with all the detailed tilework I ask you to do. Alex, thank you for being my copilot on our Vermont photography trip and being our assistant! Big thanks to my incredibly talented sister, Kristin, who loaned me her plant babies and accessories and helped me style my own home for the book. Gleni, Editor Extraordinaire, thank you for your constant encouragement, your innate sense of knowing when my brain was frazzled, and for your editorial clarity, which helped me work through my "design brain dumps." Last, but not least, thank you to my family, John, Miles, and Sebastian, who support me no matter what—even boring DIY projects at our house and cabin.

—**Karen Nepacena**

What an honor it's been to work on the creation of this book from the beginning. Thank you, Karen, for trusting me, not only to capture your brilliant designs, but also as a collaborative cohort. I'm grateful for your friendship and look forward to many more projects together. Thank you to Art Center College of Design for instilling a strong photographic foundation from which I've been able to confidently build myself as a photographer. Nate Berkus, you gave me my first taste of interior photography, and for that I will be forever grateful. And further thanks to you and Jeremiah Brent for trusting me to capture your collective vision. Kelly Engstrom, thank you for your continued championing. Thank you to Kim MacColl for your encouragement and tutelage as we navigated photographing countless catalogues, knowledge I've applied across all my photographic endeavors from interiors to portraiture. To all the homeowners who opened their doors, giving us all a peek into their lives, we all thank you! And to my dear friends, thank you for hanging in there with me as I disappear into work from time to time. You are always there with open arms when I reemerge. A huge thanks to Rich for your never-ending support and to my dad, a photographer himself, for sharing the wonder of photography with me. Lastly, thanks to my entire family who encourage and inspire me daily.

—**Christopher Dibble**

Generous gratitude to the Gibbs Smith team for seeing the potential in our project. Gleni Bartels and Ryan Thomann, thank you for being steadfast advocates and encouraging supporters throughout; Margo Tantau, we are grateful to you for bringing our initial concept to Gibbs Smith.

—CD & KN

INDEX

Karen Nepacena is known for her ability to blend beauty and practicality, solve unique design problems, and make interior design approachable for homeowners. She quickly emerged as one of the country's leading authorities on midcentury modern design when her firm, Destination Eichler, restored her family's Eichler home. Her blog of the same name chronicled the journey and captured the attention of outlets such as *Domino*, *Dwell*, *HGTV Magazine*, Apartment Therapy, and *Atomic Ranch*. Karen also has a passion for vintage pieces and DIY design projects that get the whole family involved. She lives in the San Francisco Bay Area with her husband, two sons, and rescue dog, Velvet. *Midcentury Modern Style* is her first book.

Christopher Dibble is proud to carry the photography torch forward in his family lineage. His dad and grandfather were both professional photographers in their heyday.

He's a photographer, husband, dog guy, and loves to use color in unpredictable ways that surprise and contribute to a great image. He works mostly along the West Coast and is based out of Portland, Oregon, and Los Angeles. Connecting with people and earning their trust in front of the lens is his #1 goal, capturing images that span between clean elegance and whimsical fun and land somewhere between editorial storytelling and catalogue crispness.

His work has been featured in editorial publications including *House Beautiful*, *Dwell*, HGTV, *Country Living*, *Entertainment Weekly*, *Time*, *Paper*, and *People* magazine, among others. Commercial clients include Sunbrella, the Shade Store, Framebridge, Momentum Textiles, l.a. Eyeworks and many designers, artists, and architects.